# The One Duck Revolution

## - *Why Asia does not do European farming* -

## Takao FURUNO

The 2007 Ph.D. Dissertation:

### A Comparative Study of Traditional Asian Duck Paddy Field Grazing Agriculture and Integrated Rice and Duck Farming

#### – With Reference to Farming System Theory and Focusing on the Significance of Enclosure –

Translated by Patricia Ormsby and Tony Boys

First Edition 2012

Furuno, Takao
The One-Duck Revolution

Translators: Patricia Ormsby and Tony Boys

ISBN: 978-1-300-07633-9


1. Agriculture
2. Environmental Studies

Published by Takao Furuno on Lulu.com

## Table of Contents

# Introduction: How I Got My Ph.D.

Takao Furuno

In May each year since 1998, by invitation of Professor Yokokawa, I have been giving a course in integrated rice and duck farming at Kyushu University. When I finished the course in 2005, Professor Yokokawa said to me, "Why don't you write a thesis on your integrated rice and duck farming and its connections with Asia?" At the time I replied, "Yes, OK," but in the rush of farm work after that I forgot all about it.

In May the following year, when I went to see Professor Yokokawa in his office, he asked me, "How's the Ph.D. thesis coming along?" "What Ph.D. thesis is that?" I answered. "The one we talked about last year." "Yes, I remember you mentioned a thesis, but I don't remember anything about a Ph.D." "When we say 'thesis' like that, we mean a Ph.D. thesis." "What use is a Ph.D. to a farmer like me?" "I think it would be very useful when you go to China or to other countries. You can just summarise what you have written so far and give it a bit of a new flavour."

For someone like me, who has been involved with organic farming for over 30 years, working in the fields from morning till evening, a Ph.D. seemed to be a very distant goal. I was very surprised to know that there was a way to gain a Ph.D. by submitting a thesis, making it unnecessary to enrol in a Ph.D. graduate school course. I wondered whether it was really possible for a farmer like me to write a Ph.D. thesis without taking the courses in a regular master's and Ph.D. programme.

I realized that if I were able to complete a Ph.D. thesis at roughly the same time as my children were doing their graduation papers and master's thesis it would give my children something to consider when they come to ponder what life is all about. It was thinking these thoughts that I came to write the Ph.D. thesis as the final challenge of my fifties.

I started work on the thesis from June of that year, but working on the farm from morning till evening, it was very hard for me to do both the work and write the thesis. Every morning I decided on a theme I would think about during the day as I did my work. But writing was a different matter. After working for more than 12 hours every day, it took me at least an hour of 'warming up' to switch my head from work mode to thesis mode so that I could concentrate enough to write. There just wasn't enough time.

With my wife, I participated in the Slow Food producers' conference held in Torino, Italy in November 2006. I did a presentation there on integrated rice and duck farming. Just as we arrived back at Narita Airport, my wife collapsed with 'economy class syndrome.' She was airlifted by medical helicopter to the Hokuso Hospital in Chiba Prefecture, and cared for in the intensive care facility there for 22 days. The deadline for submission of the thesis arrived while she was in the hospital. I submitted the thesis to the professors, the head referee and vice-referees, before I had time to really think through the conclusion properly. Later, I had a phone call from one of the vice-referees, Professor Manda, who said, "Mr. Furuno, I read your thesis. It's not yet at the level we require for a Ph.D. thesis." Although I had been prepared for this, it was still a disappointment. "Since you are not trying to get the Ph.D. to help you find employment, I think it is fine for you to take your time to write something you feel really satisfied about."

Professor Manda is an educator at the same time as he is a researcher. My idea was to get a Ph.D. by somehow making time during the busy working day, but I think I was in a sense running away from myself. Professor Manda's comments made me think that I needed to put a more sustained effort into the thesis and really get to grips with what I wanted to achieve personally. Until that time I think it had been arrogant and simplistic of me to think that the inherent originality of the integrated rice and duck farming method only needed summarizing to become a Ph.D. thesis. In fact, that wasn't the case at all, and the 'originality' that Professor Yokokawa had implied was the creativity to uncover 'innovative meanings' based on the work I had done up until that time, and it was Professor Manda who helped me realise that that was what I needed to do in order to write a thesis I would find personally satisfactory.

One vice-referee, Professor Eto, corrected my unsatisfactory paper with a red pen. Another vice-referee, Professor Satoshi Kai, gave me advice on the right way to write an academic paper. Yet another vice-referee, Professor Atsumu Ohnishi, later gave me rigorous advice about management analysis.

In May 2007, 50 days of intensive filming by NHK Professional began. The farming busy season, the filming and the rush to get the thesis completed all clashed and everything just became a hectic blur. Even in that busy time, I did not rest, but thought things out bit by bit and realized that the path would open up if I kept on writing. Of course, I was only able to get over this difficult period because of the support of my wife and children.

The head referee, Professor Yokokawa, guided me with great warmth from beginning to end. Writing the thesis from day to day was hard, but going to Kyushu University once a month to present my work with Professor Yokokawa listening, and then engaging in discussion took me right back to my days as a student for a very enjoyable hour or two. At these times, at Professor Yokokawa's request, my eldest son, Kotaro always attended with me. At the time, my son was studying in the Agricultural Management Science Laboratory of the Graduate School of Kyushu University. After the discussion with Professor Yokokawa, we would go to a restaurant near the university and enjoy a glass of beer while he gave me his impressions and we talked over ideas for the thesis. Although there were many problems, I think now that the year spent writing the thesis was one of the most fulfilling times of my life.

Professor Yokokawa's kind and uncomplicated "You can just summarise what you have written so far and give it a bit of a new flavour" caused me to decide to write the thesis without thinking about it too deeply. Now that I have completed the thesis, I think that without the culinary art of 'originality' I would not have been able to give the writing much flavour. Professor Yokokawa is also an educator as well as a researcher.

Many thanks.

|  |  |
|---|---|
| *Kanbai ya* | Early spring plum |
| *Gakui wo iwai* | As if to celebrate my degree |
| *Ni san rin* | Two or three blossoms |

With hands folded        Takao Furuno

# Chapter 1

## Overview and Chapter Structure

### 1-1 Overview and New Methodological Viewpoint

The integrated rice and duck farming (IRDF) method that originated in Japan is now spreading throughout the countries of Asia, and although we do not have accurate statistics, it is thought that 200,000 hectares (ha) of paddy fields were using this farming method in 2004. This is roughly equivalent to the area planted to rice in Kyushu (southern Japan) in the same year. In China's Anhui Province, alone, 50,000 people were using this method to farm 30,000 ha of land. In South Korea, 7,400 households were farming 6,300 ha using this method in 2006. The method is also spreading in Vietnam, Taiwan, the Philippines, Malaysia, Bangladesh, Myanmar, Thailand, and so on.[1]

The Chinese began to domesticate wild ducks about 3,000 years ago. Since then, ducks have been kept in many Asian countries and allowed to graze in paddy fields. Thus there has been a very long tradition of keeping ducks in paddy fields in Asia. This traditional duck paddy field grazing declined sharply in China in the 1960s and in Vietnam and the Philippines in the 1970s when chemical fertilizers and pesticides began to be used in large volumes. Subsequently, duck sheds became the main method for raising ducks in Asia. Given these circumstances, why has the Japanese IRDF method become so popular? Possible reasons are economic development, pollution of the environment, the pollution of food, agricultural policy, and so on.

So why has the 'IRDF' method and not the 'traditional duck paddy field grazing' method been spreading in these countries? In what ways do the two methods differ? This paper is an investigation of the technical differences and similarities of these two methods and clarifies the characteristic, yet universal, nature of IRDF from the viewpoint of farming system theory. Farming system theory is a means for comprehending the entire system of production technologies based on the intensification of land use practices, including crop cultivation methods, livestock farming methods, the use of agricultural tools and machinery, agricultural work procedures, and so on. Finally, I conclude that the fundamental difference between these two techniques lies in the notion of 'enclosure.'[2]

IRDF has thus far been the subject of academic research from the viewpoints of animal husbandry, soil science, biology and agricultural economics at Kagoshima University, Miyazaki University, Okayama University, Kyushu University, Fukuoka Agricultural Research Centre and the Fukuoka Prefecture Iizuka Area Agricultural Extension Centre.[3] This research has mainly been concerned with the verification and clarification of the 'duck

---

[1] See Jin [132] for cultivated areas.
[2] See Iwakata [7] for agricultural theory.
[3] See Manda et al. [87]-[116] for the outcomes of academic research.

4

effect.' This paper, while benefiting from the results of this academic research, investigates the entire technological system of IRDF from the point of view of farming system theory, and therefore represents an attempt to look at it from a new angle. Research into IRDF, including my own, has tended thus far to concentrate on comparisons with modern farming techniques. In this paper, I have conducted *diachronic* (change occurring over time) and *synchronic* (events occurring at a particular time) comparative research, in other words, historical and contemporary comparative farming system theory research, with IRDF as the pivotal feature. I have chosen as comparative models the European agricultural revolution, the development of traditional Asian agriculture, traditional Asian duck paddy field grazing, and the IRDF that is now spreading in Asia. What has become apparent from this research using farming system theory to compare IRDF with other models is an issue that has almost never arisen in comparisons with conventional modern agricultural techniques; that of 'enclosure.'

The concept of 'farming system theory' appeared in discussions in the Agricultural Economics Society of Japan from around the 1960s, and was considered an academic field that would respond to the issues of agricultural modernization. The reality of Japanese agriculture from that time, however, has been modernization through the popularization of chemical fertilizers, pesticides, herbicides, machinery, and so on. Livestock farming has moved away from being a land-use system towards livestock processing. Weed prevention and control systems, and soil fertility regeneration systems making rational use of natural forces and based on intensive land use, as proposed by farming system theory, were summarily discarded. 'Organic farming' was no exception. Professor Shigeru Yasuda has defined organic farming in the following way: "Organic farming is a generic name for agriculture that endeavours to maintain productivity by basing the circulation of matter in the relationships between land – crops – (livestock) – and humans on the principles of natural cycles, and renouncing the environment- and life-destroying characteristics inherent in modern agriculture" (p.140). The reality is, however, that it is not unusual to find that pesticides have simply been replaced by natural materials, organic materials have been substituted for chemical fertilizers, with no change whatever in the basic structure of reliance upon external inputs. The fundamental problem is lack of a conceptual viewpoint informed by notions of farming systems. I believe that the contemporary significance of farming system theory remains as great as it ever was.[4]

## 1-2 Chapter Structure

Chapter 2 will clarify the special technical features of IRDF and show that the concept of 'integration' is a universal concept that complements the basic traditional farming practice of 'rotation.'

Following that, I will describe the technical structure of IRDF. It will become clear that all

---

[4] See Morita [84] for a viewpoint based on farming systems.

these techniques unfold from the basic notion of 'enclosure.' Thus, mainly by comparing them with modern agricultural techniques, I hope to clarify the technical characteristics of IRDF and the comprehensive and integrated nature of the techniques, as well as the techniques for the expanded use of resources, the techniques that give rise to the diverse productive powers of paddy fields and so on.

In the end, IRDF, a creative union of rice farming and animal husbandry, forms a technological construct that differs completely from modern agricultural technology. This description of the special characteristics of IRDF is a cognitive frame of reference for understanding the content of this publication from Chapter 3 on.

In Chapter 3, I will probe into the position and significance of IRDF from the viewpoint of farming systems by comparing the European agricultural revolution and the development of traditional Asian agriculture. My intention here is to take a wide perspective by comparing IRDF with technological systems that centre on land use in order to clarify its particular characteristics as well as its universality.

IRDF benefits from the labour-saving Three Phase Method and Grain-Grass Method, and it can also be regarded as an 'integrated' technological system that simultaneously implements the Rotational Cultivation Method's weed prevention and control while maintaining soil fertility in Asian paddy fields. In short, IRDF is an integrated technological system that incorporates both the 'energy-saving nature' of the animal power of the European agricultural revolution and the diversity of traditional Asian agriculture.

In Chapter 4, I present a number of cases of traditional Asian duck paddy field grazing based on my observation and experiences, a questionnaire survey, and other materials I have collected. In Asia, domesticated ducks are allowed to graze freely in unenclosed paddy fields. This used to be the standard method of raising ducks in Asia. Its purpose was to fatten up the ducks rather than to confer positive impacts on the rice plants. Nevertheless, its effects of insect removal, weeding, intertillage, and so on have been recognized since ancient times.

Chapter 5 will discuss the current state of IRDF and its current spread throughout Asia based on my own interview surveys and the results of a questionnaire survey carried out in several countries. The relevant natural, social and historical conditions in Asia - in Japan, South Korea, China, Vietnam, Cambodia, the Philippines, Indonesia, Malaysia, India and Bangladesh - are subtly different. When IRDF is introduced into these differing environments, for example as with the trend towards large-scale farming in China, collective farming in South Korea, and the shift towards livestock farming in Vietnam, a diversity of development trajectories are seen depending on the conditions in each country.

Chapter 6 forms the conclusion. In Chapters 2 and 3, a comparison of the techniques of traditional Asian duck paddy field grazing and IRDF was attempted from the viewpoints of farming system theory and the techniques used. I firstly showed that the difference in technique between traditional Asian duck paddy field grazing and IRDF is 'enclosure.' I then looked at the significance of the enclosed paddy field from the viewpoint of farming system theory in terms of constituent factors bearing on agricultural productivity and show that it is a "container-like labour device." In other words, in IRDF, the "container-like labour device" created by enclosing the paddy field makes possible and enhances the beneficial activities of the "animal power labour device" – the ducks.

Further, concerning each of the six effects of ducks on rice plants mentioned in Chapter 2, I consider the principles that govern the manner in which the existence of the enclosure influences the mechanism of the technology.

In conclusion, traditional Asian duck paddy field grazing has for the first time undergone a synthetic development into a full-fledged rice cultivation technology by evolving into IRDF through the enclosure of paddy fields.

The final chapter, Chapter 7, shows how the significance of enclosure, which is not apparent simply through a conventional comparison with modern agricultural techniques, has come to light through the research methodology of diachronic and synchronic comparative research into IRDF, as show in this dissertation.

# Chapter 2
# Characteristics of the Integrated Rice and Duck Farming (IRDF) Technology

## 2-1 Introduction

In February 1988, I received a memo from Suemitsu Nomiyama, a leader in natural farming methods who lives in Inatsuki Town, the town adjacent to mine, regarding a "duck weeding method" used by the late Toshio Okita, a natural farming practitioner in Toyama Prefecture. That summer, following the advice of the memo, I released several four-week-old ducklings into a paddy field with a net enclosure. Incredibly, the weeds in that paddy field disappeared.

For ten years prior to that, I had been practicing organic farming without using synthetic agricultural chemicals. I tried all manner of weed elimination methods. I rotated between rice and vegetable fields, tried deep-water cultivation, double ploughing and muddying, releasing young carp, releasing tadpole shrimp, introducing electric powered weeding machines… No matter what I did, the weeds defeated me. In that situation you can imagine how amazed and delighted I was at the ability of ducks to eliminate weeds. That memo from Toshio Okita was the starting point of my involvement with IRDF.

While I was still enjoying my success, however, in the dog days of August, wouldn't you know it, three feral dogs attacked the ducks in my paddy fields. I called Mr. Okita. He said, "You can't use this method where there are a lot of dogs." I was terribly disappointed, but I had no other choice, so I plucked up my courage and began a battle against feral dogs. The next year I set up a cucumber net within the paddy field, two meters from the levee, then I set up a tough *nori* net (used in cultivating seaweed) so that it hung down in an 'L' shape on the levee. I suffered a string of defeats. Days battling tooth and nail against the dogs biting and killing my ducks continued.

Then, one day during the rainy season of the third year, in late June to early July, I was out in the mountains in a Japanese cedar (*Cryptomeria japonica*) forest and I chanced upon an electric fence installed in a clearing to protect a taro field from wild boars. I immediately thought of adopting it to protect my duck paddy field. I tried it and it worked excellently, and from that day forward, feral dogs ceased to bother my ducks. As I was watching my ducks swimming around freely, it occurred to me that they were not merely a weed-elimination method, but that the rice and the ducks were growing up together in the paddy field. At this juncture, at the suggestion of the late photographer Mamoru Iwashita, I teamed up with Mitsuyasu Noai, an agricultural extension officer, to perform a comparative survey of the multi-faceted influence of the ducks on the rice plants by setting up a 3 meter by 3 meter square "control plot" within the paddy field. We found differences between the area with ducks and the duck-free control plot in terms of the types and numbers of weeds, numbers of insect pests, growth and volume of yield of rice plants and the condition of the soil. Since then, I have continued creating technology that is both theoretical and practical for IRDF, using a trial-and-error approach in the paddy fields.

IRDF is a technology in which two kinds of living things, a plant (rice) and an animal (ducks) are raised at the same time in the same space. This system differs fundamentally from that of modern agricultural technology, in which only one item is being grown. It also differs from what we usually refer to as traditional agricultural technology, in which crops are rotated or multiple crops are raised for subsistence.

### 2-1-(1) Defining IRDF

I do not know of a scholarly definition of "IRDF." I coined the term "IRDF" myself.

One week after planting the rice seedlings (or if the seeds are directly sown, about 23 days after sowing), an enclosure of netting and/or electric fencing is set up and about 15 to 30 ducklings per ten ares (one-tenth of a hectare) are released into this enclosure about a week after they hatch.

The ducks eat the weeds and insect pests in the paddy field along with feed provided, and their droppings provide nutrition for the rice plants. The ducks and rice plants are raised simultaneously in a mutually prosperous manner. This technological system, which creatively integrates rice production and livestock raising, is defined as "IRDF."

The rice and the ducks are like classmates, raised together in the paddy field.

Rather than say we are growing rice in the paddy field, it is more accurate to say that we are raising rice and livestock simultaneously in the same paddy field.

The objective is not merely to use the ducks to help grow rice; equal value is put on both the rice and the ducks.

It is hard to express this integrated technology in terms of previously conceived ideas. In the history of rice production in Japan, rice was considered the main crop, and after its harvest an off-season crop of onions, potatoes, wheat or other winter crops might be grown in the paddy field during the interval before the next rice planting. Rice was always the "master" crop and the winter crops were considered secondary or subordinate.

I therefore wondered how best to express this technology for raising rice together with ducks, and I came up with the concept of "integrated farming." Not a "main crop" or "winter crop," but a "simultaneous crop." That's how I came to coin the term "IRDF."

In a broad sense, the way duck farmers breed ducks in Indonesia, Vietnam and China, in which harvested paddy fields are enclosed and the ducks are released into these already-harvested paddy fields, might be considered a form of IRDF. However, what I am calling "IRDF" here is only the method in which ducks are released into a paddy field while the rice plants are growing, with the rice and ducks being raised together.

### 2-1-(2) The concept of integrated farming

IRDF is an experience-based or empirical technology. In order to reformulate this empirical technology into a theoretical one, we should first focus on the general concept of "integrated farming." The revolutionary nature of "integrated farming" can be elucidated by contrasting it with "rotational cultivation," a basic principle of traditional agriculture.

"Rotational cultivation" is a method of growing different kinds of crops on the same land following a certain order of crop combinations over time to avoid reduced land productivity and outbreaks of disease and insect pests that occur on repeatedly cultivated soil, and is a basic principle in traditional farming.

In contrast, "integrated farming" is a synchronic agricultural production method for the cultivation of rice plants and ducks (and with enough practical experience, fish such as loaches). In other words, plants and animals are enclosed in a defined space, their balance and internal relationships being maintained so that they are raised simultaneously in a mutually prosperous manner. As Figure 2-1 shows, rotational cultivation is a diachronic system, while integrated farming is a synchronic system. A comprehensive look at both systems will clarify the significance of integrated farming.

From the viewpoint of the "time" axis, rotational cultivation consists of an orderly succession of crops, different crops mainly being planted at different times as in the vertical flow of time shown in Figure 2-1. On the other hand, integrated farming involves internal relationships between different crops or between crops and livestock within the same space at the same time, represented horizontally in the figure. In other words, as Figure 2-1 shows, integrated farming is a broad concept with a complementary relationship to rotational farming. By defining the concept of integrated farming and utilizing it this way, we can reformulate the empirical technology of IRDF into a theoretical concept. Traditional "mixed cropping" and "intercropping" were forms of integrated cropping involving relationships between different plants, so we can also consider IRDF to be an integrated cropping system involving a relationship between plants and animals.

**Figure 2-1. Relationship between Rotational Cultivation and Integrated Farming**

"Rotational Cultivation" → (Diachronic)

"Integrated/Simultaneous Farming → (Synchronic)

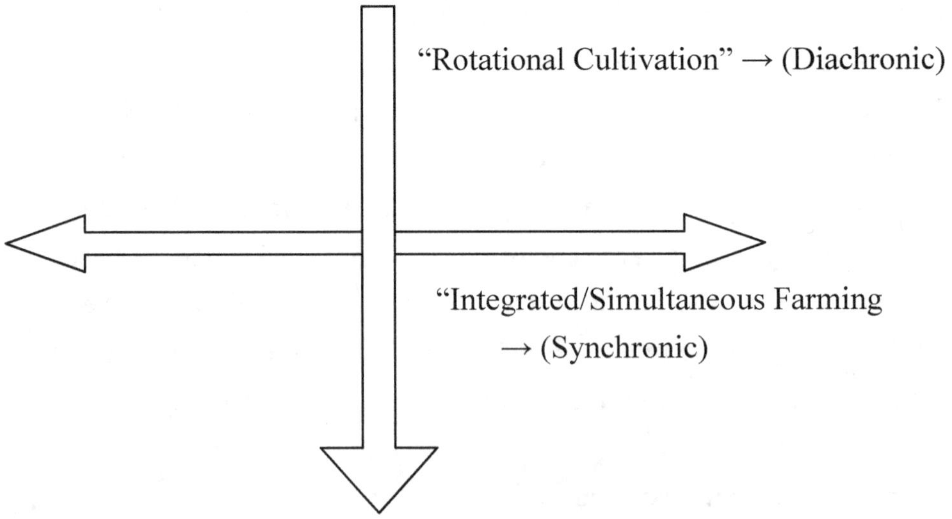

Source: Prepared by the author.

Rice farming is a form of repetitive agriculture in which continuous cultivation of the same crop is carried out in the same soil at the same time each year. Integrated farming arose within rice farming, adding the technique of enclosure. In other words, starting from repeated cultivation, the traditional upland farming technique of rotational cultivation was discovered, and based upon traditional simultaneous farming techniques of mixed cropping and intercropping, "integrated farming" was rediscovered in paddy field rice farming by adding an enclosure.[5]

## 2-2 Structure of IRDF Technology

### 2-2-(1) Everything started with enclosure

A prerequisite for IRDF technology is an enclosure. A paddy field in which the rice seedlings are growing is enclosed by netting or an electric fence and the ducklings are released into this well-defined space. This is where it all starts.

In research carried out to date, including my own, too much attention has been paid to comparisons with modern technology, so the significance of enclosure has been considered self-evident and not studied in depth.

The importance of enclosure becomes apparent when we make an extensive study of traditional Asian duck paddy field grazing, in which the ducks are released to wander freely in paddy fields without enclosures, and IRDF.

The entire technological structure of IRDF described below was developed on the basis of enclosure.

### 2-2-(2) Overall characteristics of the technology

So-called environmentally-friendly rice farming (using tadpole shrimp [*Triopus longicaudatus*], golden snails, carp, rice bran, paper mulch, deep water flooding, winter flooding) is basically a weed control technology. Because of this, there is a tendency to view IRDF as just another technology for weed control. IRDF, however, is much more than a weed control technology. It is a comprehensive technological system.[6]

As Figure 2-1 above shows, within this technological system, the duck community and the plant community comprise a realm in which comprehensive and mutual effects are produced. This technology is a creative union of rice farming and livestock breeding, in which the paddy field is a complete ecosystem. Within that, the ducks are at the same time a means and an objective. The ducks perform the following six tasks for the rice plants:

(1) Weeding

(2) Pest control

(3) Nutrient supply

(4) Full-time ploughing and muddying

---

[5] See Nakaoka [32] for more on the concepts of diachronic and synchronic systems.

[6] See Civil Rice Farming Research Centre [79] for more on rice farming without herbicides.

(5) Stimulation

(6) Golden snail control

**Figure 2-2. The technological system of IRDF**

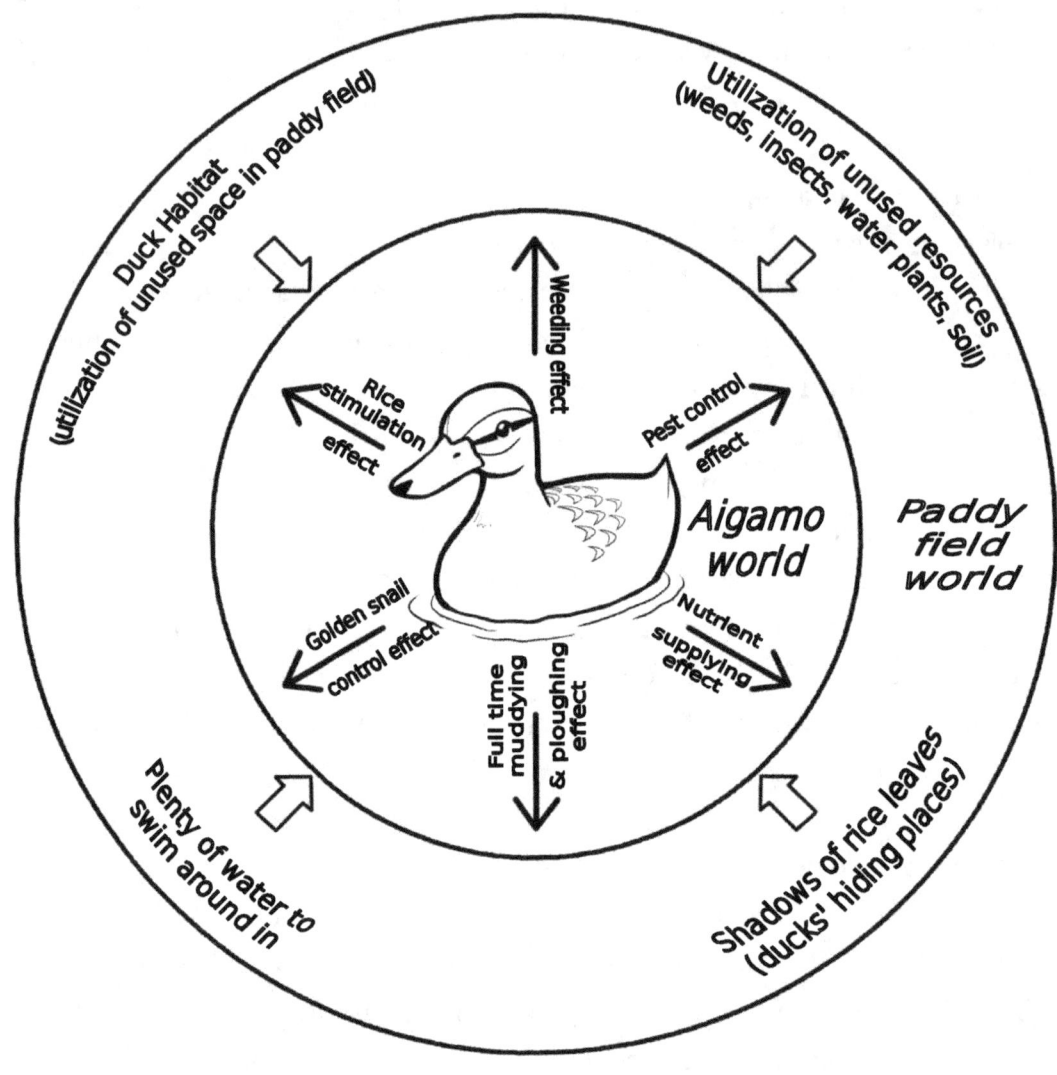

Source: Takao Furuno, *Aigamo Banzai*, p. 16. [44]

In actual practice, these six duck effects are realized in a comprehensive, simultaneous and homogenous manner. The paddy field, in return, has the following three influences on (i.e., provides the following benefits to) the ducks:

(1) Provision of unused resources – a supply of fodder such as fallen rice ears, weeds and weed seeds, pests, aquatic organisms, and so on.

(2) Provision of unused space – abundant water and living space.

(3) Provision of cover – protection from predators and shade from the direct rays of the summer sun.

In recent years, a plant called azolla (see section 2-2-(7) for details on azolla), and fish have been added to the IRDF system, transforming the paddy fields into an ever more productive space.[7]

## 2-2-(3) Overall features of the technology

Figure 2-3 compares IRDF with modernized rice farming technology.

The modernized rice farming technologies currently being used in most rice paddies are herbicides for weed control, pesticides for pest and disease control, and chemical fertilizers for nutrient supply, as shown in Figure 2-3. In other words, each source of trouble is dealt with by different means. This combination of separate ways of handling problems is characteristic of modernized rice farming technology. Furthermore, the pesticides, herbicides and chemical fertilizers are all petroleum-derived industrial products.

In IRDF, on the other hand, the ducks handle all the tasks of weeding, pest control, nutrient supply, and moreover of ploughing & muddying, stimulation and golden snail control all by themselves. I call this the integrated technology of "one duck—myriad blessings." This point is where it differs fundamentally from modern rice farming technology.

Note that in Figure. 2-3, the rows are empty for ploughing & muddying and stimulation effects in modern rice farming technology. This is because these two functions are not a part of mainstream modern rice farming technology.

In the 1950s and earlier, farmers ploughed and weeded using weeding machines pushed through the paddy fields by hand. Since then, convenient herbicides have eliminated the need to perform the hard work of pushing weeding machines or pulling weeds by hand under the blazing sun. However, plant hormone researcher Yasuo Ohta had the following to say as long as twenty years ago, "One example of the active use of contact stimulation in agriculture was in the raising of healthy rice plants. In Japan's northeastern region and in mountainous Nagano Prefecture, there was a traditional technique passed down of stroking the rice plant leaves each morning with bamboo brooms or poles to sweep away the dew hanging from the tips of the leaves. The rice plants received physical stimulation, the result of which was that they produced ethylene and grew into strong healthy plants."[12]

---

[7] See Furuno [45], pp. 12-18 for more on the overall technology.

**Figure 2-3. A Comparison of IRDF and Modernized Rice Farming Technology**

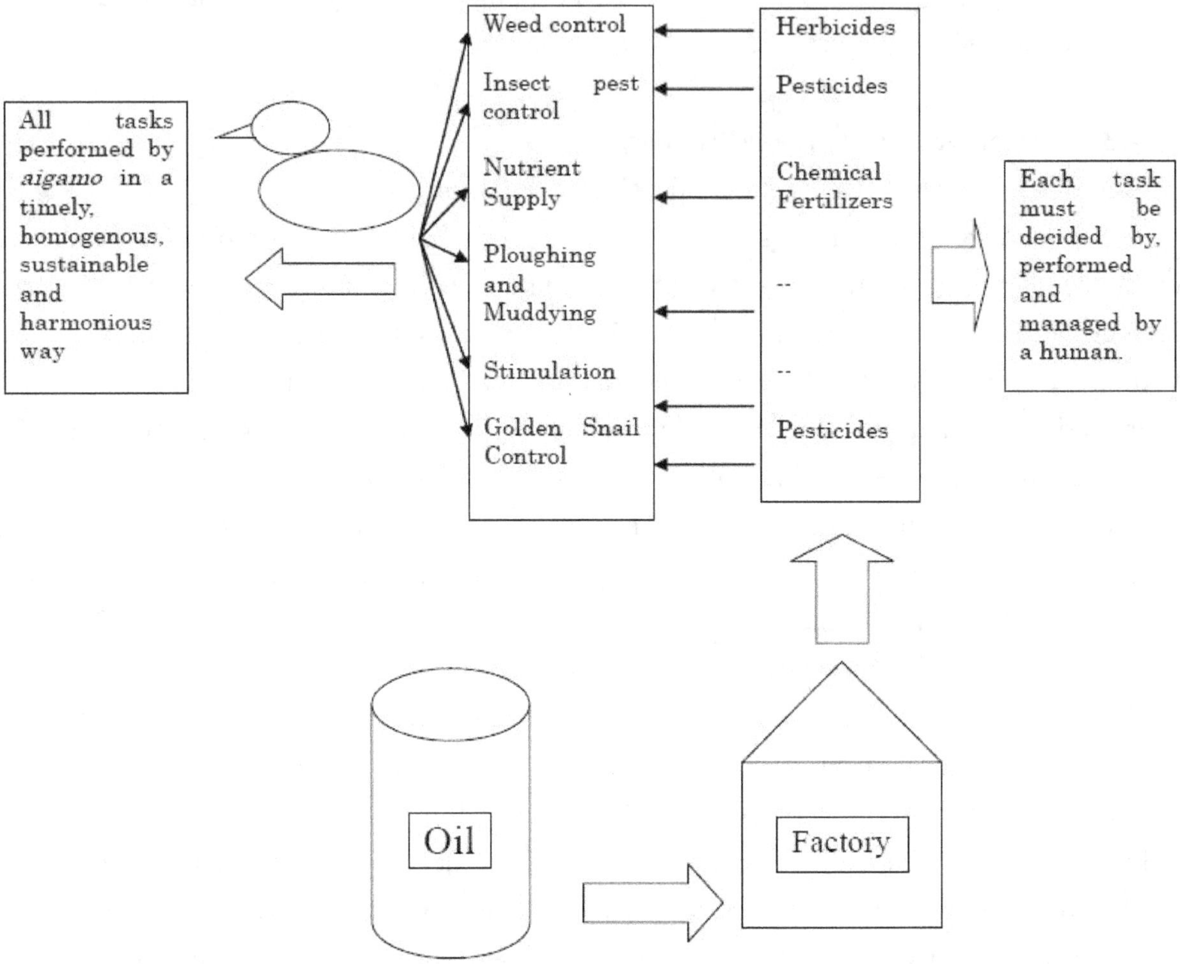

Source: Prepared by the author.

Developed through experience, IRDF is a realistic method that actively applies direct stimulation not only at the seedling production stage, as noted by Ohta above, but also later on when the seedlings are transplanted into the large paddy fields. From the time the ducklings are released into the paddy fields in the second week after planting until they are removed from the paddy field, they poke at the bases of the rice plants, providing stimulation. In modern rice farming, it would be difficult to provide this kind of stimulation on a regular basis using machines.

Historically, prior to the 1950s, when most rice farmers used weeding machines to control weeds, the stimulation effect was a factor noticed and recognized through experience in ploughing and weeding operations. In modern rice farming, however, farmers have become completely dependent on the convenience of herbicides and have utterly forgotten about the stimulation factor. This is one factor that can be appreciated anew in IRDF.

In modern rice farming, no matter how convenient the pesticides, herbicides and chemical fertilizers, it is the farmer who must choose the appropriate time for applying them. By the same token, though a machine may do most of the work, it is still the farmer who must operate it. In IRDF, the duck performs all the work of weeding, pest control, nutrient supply, stimulation, and so on, and moreover at the appropriate times without instruction, eliminating the need for meticulous management. Of course, some labour is necessary on the livestock breeding side of the operation, but overall, no excessively heavy labour is required. If the ducklings are released into the paddy fields at the right time, both the ducks and rice plants will grow up together naturally. This technological feature represents a major difference from modern rice farming.

From this standpoint, IRDF creatively and directly utilizes the energy of livestock, which functions as a substitute for petroleum energy. This is wonderful beyond words.

Energy use has progressed from manpower to livestock power to fossil fuel energy. In modern society, almost all work, including that of agriculture, is accomplished using energy from oil. However, if livestock energy is creatively harnessed, it can achieve benefits that go beyond its function as a mere substitute for oil. This is the potential of the energy inherent in life.[8]

## 2-2-(4) Increasing resource utilization

Nothing in nature exists without a purpose. All living things in the Earth's ecosystems have been given their own individual role, which they perform actively until they die. The weeds and pests in a paddy field are no exception.

On occasion I use the terms "weed," "beneficial plant," "pest," "beneficial insect," and "just an insect," but are these definitions really fixed?

Certainly, in monoculture rice farming, where only rice plants are supposed to grow in the paddy fields, weeds are weeds and pests are pests. However, the situation is different when rice farming and livestock breeding are conducted concurrently in a polyculture, such as in IRDF.

Once we release amphibious ducks, which eat both weeds and insect pests and which can live both on land and water, the situation changes completely, instantly shattering our preconceived notions. The weeds and pests that were formerly villains become an important source of food for the ducks, their flesh and blood, and then they become nutrients for the rice plants. What is epoch-making about this technology is that weeds and pests, considered nuisances throughout the 2000-year history of rice farming, in integrated farming are now considered resources (fodder for ducks), a forward-thinking transformation,.

In the monocultures of modernized rice farming, all focus seems to stop at the relationship between humans and rice plants, and weeds and pests are deemed villains or nuisances, with continuous efforts made to kill and thus "control" them with pesticides and herbicides. Didn't anybody ever get the idea of making positive use of weeds and pests as resources? A typical example of the former way of thinking can be seen in Junichi Sakai's *Agricultural Resource Economics Theory*, published by the Association of Agricultural and Forestry Statistics.

---

[8] See Furuno [43] for more on the creative utilization of animal power energy.

Incidentally, I would like to note that the present thesis does not examine the concept of "resources" itself, but rather focuses on the state of technology for the utilization of un-utilized or under-utilized resources. In his book, Professor Sakai stipulates that resources consist of useful natural things [141]. Based on this stipulation, it can be said that weeds and pests become resources utilized by the technology of IRDF. In conventional cultivation practices, weeds and pests are not considered useful natural things, so they are not perceived as resources. Therefore, mainstream agriculture is incapable of considering weeds and pests as resources.

Weeds and pests are by no means permanent categories. They change in accordance with the state of technology being applied. IRDF is not so much a weed and pest control technique as a "technological system for the positive utilization of weeds and pests." In other words, resources are seen as a relative phenomenon. This is the originality of integrated farming, which encompasses rice farming and livestock breeding. The change in perspective is the crucial factor.[9]

On a further note, IPM (Integrated Pest Management) technology is also used for controlling pests and diseases, the larger environment being taken into consideration while productivity is maintained. Figure 2-4 gives an outline of IPM.

Within the framework of Figure 2-4, ducks would be considered "natural enemies," or a biological control method. Ducks are predatory birds. The use of birds as natural enemies, however, is not one of the major techniques of IPM.[10] Because birds can fly, their scope of action is too large, and unlike spiders, they do not make a single field their home. I will go into more detail on this in Chapter 6, but "enclosure" opened up an avenue for the utilization of birds as natural enemies. Moreover, while being natural enemies, ducks are at the same time "products." This is the real value of integrated farming, with its creative unification of livestock breeding and rice farming.

When I was establishing the technology of IRDF, I read a lot of material about the biology of rice plant pests written by entomologists applying IPM. Without a clear grasp of rice plant pest biology, I would have been unable to establish the technology for using ducks to control (or rather, use) pests.

---

[9] See Furuno [43] For more how to view weeds and pests,.

[10] See Yano [118], Nakasuji [33], Nemoto [35] or Kiriya [22] for further details.

**Figure 2-4. Outline of Integrated Pest Management (IPM)**

| Insect pest control technology | Control methods not using pesticides | **Physical control** (hot water sterilization, etc.) | → | **Selection of a combination of these methods for appropriate control.** | → | **Management of pest problems so that they fall below the acceptable level of economic losses.** |
| | | **Biological control** (natural enemies, beneficial microorganisms, etc.) | | | | |
| | | **Agronomic control** (breeding of resistant varieties, etc.) | | | | |
| | Chemical control methods (pesticides, etc.) | | | | | |
| Outbreak prevention methods (Forecasting of timing and size of outbreak based on meteorological information and so on.) | | | → | | | |

Source: Ministry of Agriculture, Forestry and Fisheries, Agriculture, Forestry and Fisheries Research Council website, Agriculture, Forestry and Fisheries R&D Report – Integrated Pest Management Technology –) http://www.s.affrc.go.jp/docs/e/index.htm

## 2-2-(5) Building diverse paddy field productivity

What sort of places are paddy fields perceived to be? This is the basic issue with regard to the existence of the technology. In the more familiar modern technology, regardless of whether we are growing rice plants, vegetables or fruit trees, the objective from the start is to produce that one item only, and the technology is set up for that purpose (monoculture).

In IRDF, however, the objective from the start is "integrated farming" in which several living things, i.e., rice plants, ducks and fish, are raised in balance in the same place (the enclosed space), while maintaining a mutual internal relationship. Thus the frameworks of these respective technologies are fundamentally different.

The perception that a rice paddy is a place for producing only rice is such an established part of rice farming's long history that it is considered common sense in Japan. The development of modern agriculture and its infrastructure were based on this way of thinking. For example, individual paddy fields were enlarged for the purpose of increasing the efficiency of agricultural machinery such as tractors, seedling planters and combines. Of course, another objective was to allow paddy fields to be dried, making it easier to grow winter crops and engage in crop rotation.

**Figure 2-5. Diverse productivity of a paddy field**

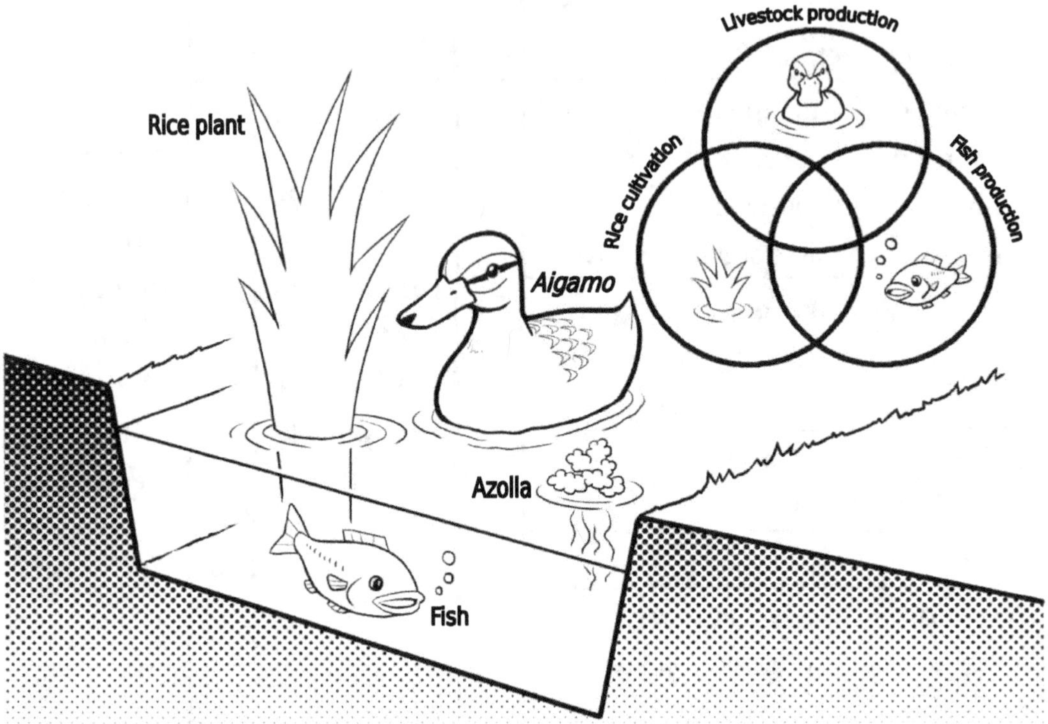

Source: Takao Furuno, *Mugen ni Hirogaru Aigamo Suito Dojisaku* (IRDF Expanding Toward Infinity), p. 85. [43]

I was born in 1950, but it wasn't until 1994 when I saw paddy fields in the Red River delta in Vietnam that I realized how narrow Japan's view of agriculture was. Not only was rice being raised, but at the same time, fish, shrimp and mud snails, which the people consumed as part of their everyday diet. Asia's rice paddies had traditionally always supported this kind of diverse productivity. Until the 1950s, Japan's paddy fields had also been the same way.

In IRDF, paddy fields are considered places for producing not only rice, but also flavourful items to be eaten with rice. It creatively combines rice farming with livestock breeding and aquaculture, based on a perspective that focuses on a re-evaluation and integration of the inherent productivity of paddy fields. In September, which is early autumn in Japan, the rice plants have turned golden in my paddy field. The ducks have fattened up and I can catch loaches or pick figs on the levees. In other words, from one paddy field, we can obtain rice, high-protein side dishes and dessert. This illustrates the diverse productivity of the paddy field. In the adjacent paddy fields where modernized rice farming is practiced, only rice plants are grown. It is clear that our perception of rice paddies as an agricultural space is important.[11]

When the diverse productivity of paddy fields is developed through rice farming, livestock breeding and aquaculture, the original biodiversity and multi-faceted functions seem to

---

[11] See Furuno [79] for more on the diverse productivity of paddy fields.

evolve as well. As I will explain later, when loach fry are released into a duck paddy field, something interesting occurs. The number of crucian carp (*Carassius carassius*) fry increases. Bill Mollison, the originator of Permaculture, said, "What is important in regard to biodiversity is not how many component elements a system has, but rather the number of functional relationships among those elements. The aim is to create a grouping of mutually compatible elements (plants, animals, buildings, etc.) which work together harmoniously." [91]

### 2-2-(6) Enhancing biodiversity

Common sense tells us that if we release ducks into a rice paddy they will eat everything in sight, impoverishing the ecosystem, but my own observations have shown me that this is not necessarily the case. Natural mechanisms are more resilient than we assume. If we release the ducklings into the paddy field when the rice seedlings are still small, there is no cover, so we see a tendency for the organisms that inhabit the aerial part of plants, including insect pests, to decrease to the point of impoverishment. However, once the rice plants have grown up and have more leaves, we see the numbers of spiders and other creatures increase.

**Figure 2-6. Numbers of spiders in a plot with ducks and a control plot**

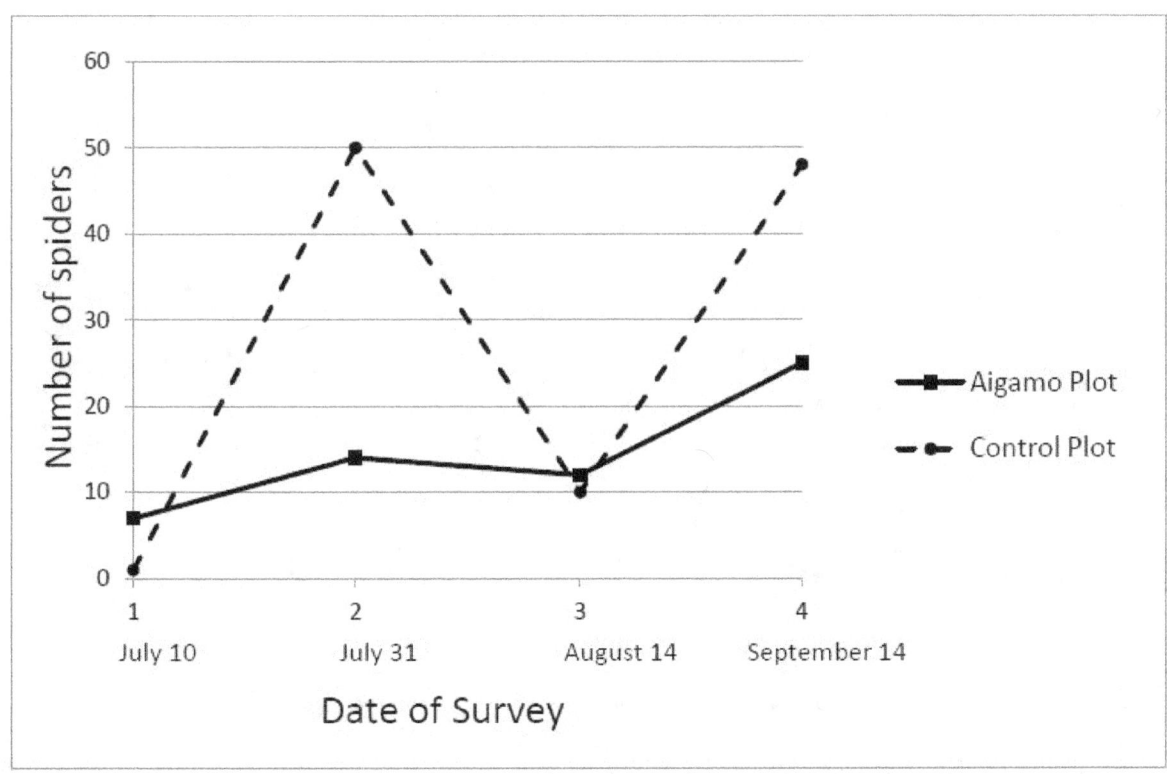

Source: Shinji Suenobu, Iizuka Area Agricultural Extension Centre), p. 98.

Figure 2-6 shows the results of a survey of spider numbers. As far as this figure shows, the number of spiders in the duck plot does not tend to be fewer than in the control plot (a 3m ×

3m space netted off so that ducks cannot enter). One or two weeks after planting, there is a great increase in the numbers of water fleas, tubificid worms, tadpole shrimp, fairy shrimp, striped diving beetles and other organisms. When the ducklings are released into the fields, they feed on these organisms. I have not done a survey to find out how many they are eating, but every year there are large numbers of these organisms. This demonstrates the flexibility of the natural world.

It is known that wild shoveller ducks eat water fleas. While it is not known whether *aigamo* ducks eat water fleas or not, the number of water fleas in paddy fields with ducks are observed to be overwhelmingly greater than in surrounding paddy fields without ducks. Figure 2-7 shows the trends in the numbers of water fleas measured by Kagoshima University researchers.

In duck paddy fields, there are large numbers of water fleas. It is thought that manure from the ducks provides them nutrients, leading to large numbers of these insects.

**Figure 2-7. Trends in numbers of water fleas**

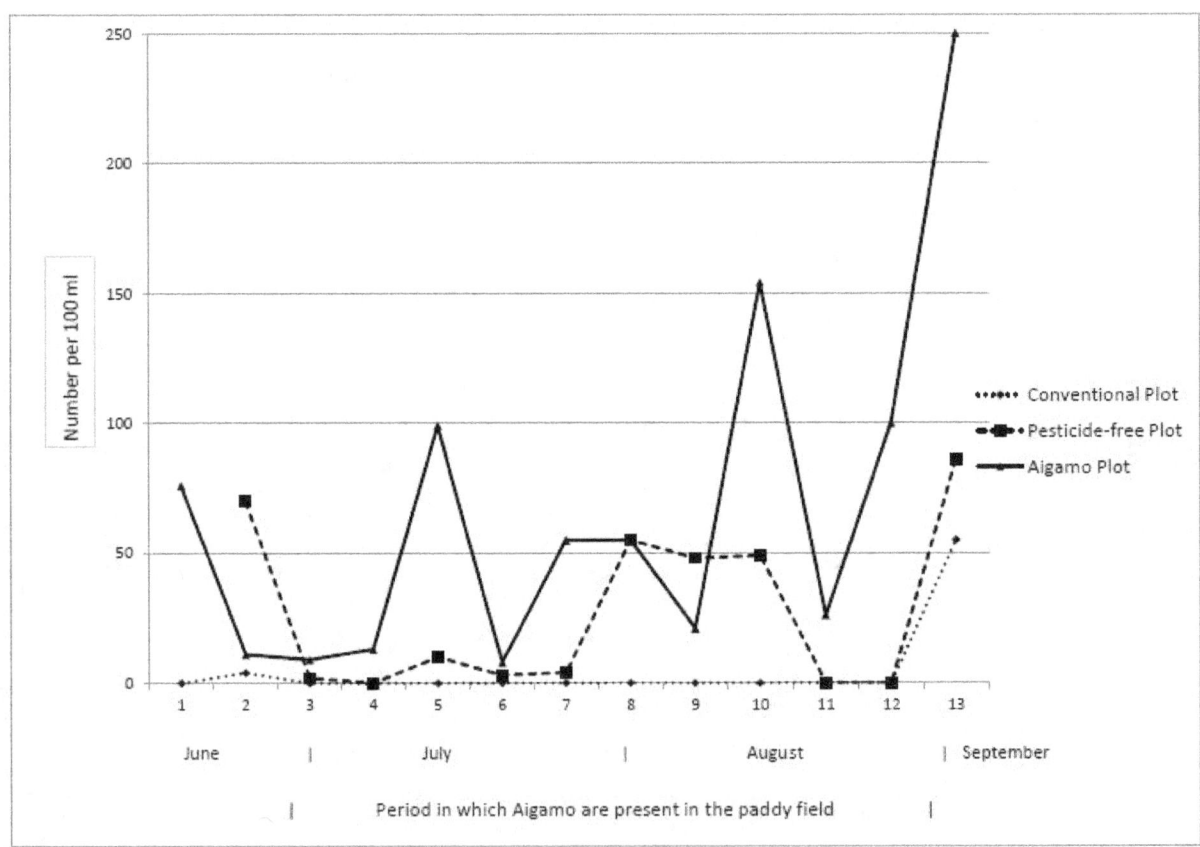

Source: Yumi Shimada and Masanori Sato, Kagoshima University, p. 93

Large numbers of tubificid worms also occur in paddy fields inhabited by ducks. I have not actually confirmed this through surveys, but it was clear from my observations. This is probably the result of the nutrients supplied by the ducks' droppings. When a duck's gastrointestinal tract is dissected, several hundred tubificid worms are found. The ducks eat the tubificid worms and in return provide nutrients via their faeces, which then support large numbers of tubificid worms. It seems that a cyclical structure has developed.

Generally, a trend is seen in which the more diverse the crops introduced into a paddy field, say progressing from rice plants alone to rice plus ducks, to rice plus ducks plus azolla, to rice plus ducks plus azolla plus loaches, the greater its overall biodiversity becomes, with larger quantities and varieties of organisms.

For example, when azolla and loaches are added to a duck paddy field, the numbers of other fish, such as crucian carp, dace and catfish show a clear increase. In 2002, when I drained the water from a paddy field with rice plants, ducks, azolla and loaches, I obtained 400 roundly fattened naturally occurring crucian carp. That year I happened to take an accurate count of the number of crucian carp, but every year I have observed hundreds of these fish making their way into my paddy fields with rice plants, ducks, azolla and loaches. *Aigamo* paddy fields have a rich aquatic ecosystem.

Agriculture originated from the premise of reversing the natural trend toward biodiversity. If we take the example of rice farming, the paddy fields are neatly tilled and only planted with rice seedlings, so that from the start an ecosystem with only one element, a plant, is created and weeds are excluded. The reason why weeds and pests thrive there is that ecosystems naturally progress from a state of simplicity to one of complexity. The task in agriculture is to suppress this natural tendency. What, therefore, is the significance of IRDF having rice plants, ducks, azolla and loaches coexisting in a paddy field? This technology differs from rice monoculture technology in that it requires us to think about biodiversity from a variety of standpoints.[12]

## 2-2-(7) Cycling atmospheric nitrogen

In 1993, I received a letter from Professor Iwao Watanabe, formerly of Mie University, asking me if I'd be interested in introducing azolla into my paddy fields, so from 1994 I began to research the use of azolla in IRDF.

Three to four weeks after releasing the ducks into the paddy fields, the weeds diminish noticeably. This is the result of the ducks' predisposition to eat the weeds, and it is convenient for the rice farmer, but not for the ducks (livestock), because for them it means insufficient green fodder. Azolla resolves that contradiction.

Azolla is a floating plant, an aquatic fern. It uses cyanobacteria, a symbiotic kind of blue-green algae, to fix nitrogen from the atmosphere. It has a superior ability to fix nitrogen; under optimal conditions, it can fix two kilograms of nitrogen per day per hectare. At the same time, azolla has a great ability to reproduce, doubling in mass in just three days under optimal conditions.

When azolla is introduced into a paddy field as duck fodder, it resolves the weeding

---

[12] See Furuno [73] for more on the biodiversity of paddy fields with ducks.

contradiction. Moreover, since azolla is a floating plant it does not compete with the rice plants for nutrients or sunlight.

Nitrogen fixed from the atmosphere via azolla passes through the ducks and from there to the rice plants and humans. Figure 2-8 illustrates this relationship. I learned a lot about azolla from Professor Iwao Watanabe.

## 2-2-(8) Productive use of aquatic space

The organisms living in modern rice paddies differ greatly from those of the 1950s. Those currently found in abundance in paddy fields, such as tadpole shrimp, fairy shrimp and golden snails, were not found in the paddy fields of the past. In the 1950s, there were instead a variety of fish and other creatures, including loaches, crucian carp, catfish, shrimp and mud snails. Today's paddy fields have a relatively simpler biota.

Almost no fish are seen in modern paddy fields. One reason for this is pollution from the pesticides, herbicides and chemical fertilizers. It seems, however, that these pollution effects have decreased recently because newer pesticides and herbicides have been developed that are less toxic to fish.

A second reason for the disappearance of fish lies in the infrastructure. Ditches are lined on three sides with concrete to separate incoming irrigation water from drainage water, and this produces an environment in which fish cannot live. Moreover, in the course of improving drainage, differences in height have been introduced between paddy fields and drainage ditches and between the ditches and the rivers into which they discharge. Additionally, when heavy rains come the gates of the drainage ditches are closed for flood prevention. For that reason, during the rainy season, fish are unable to reach the paddy fields to spawn.

In the 1950s, there were lots of loaches everywhere throughout the paddy fields and ditches. After these improvements to the infrastructure, though, they disappeared completely. I began releasing loach fry into my duck paddy field in 1996 for the purpose of restoring loaches to Japan's rice paddies.

The ducks eat fallen rice ears, weeds and pests and also the azolla, which fixes atmospheric nitrogen. At the same time, their droppings provide nutrients for tubificid worms and plankton such as rotifers and water fleas, resulting in large numbers of these organisms, which in turn feed the loaches. Then the loaches' excretions also provide nutrients to the rice plants. In this way, the rice plants, azolla, loaches and ducks form a cyclical system of mutual interdependencies in IRDF.

## Figure 2-8. Nitrogen circulation in IRDF with azolla

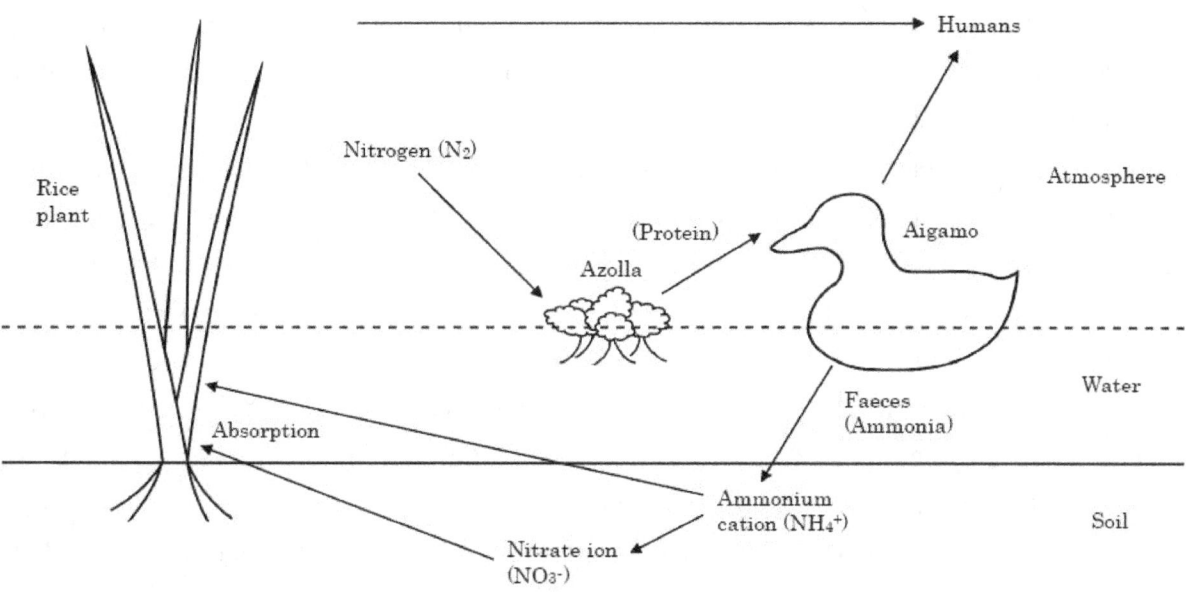

Source: Takao Furuno, IRDF Expanding Toward Infinity, p. 67. [43]

Figure 2-9 illustrates the material cycle of the ducks, rice, azolla and loaches in IRDF.[13, 14]

## Figure 2-9. Duck, rice plant, azolla and loach materials cycle

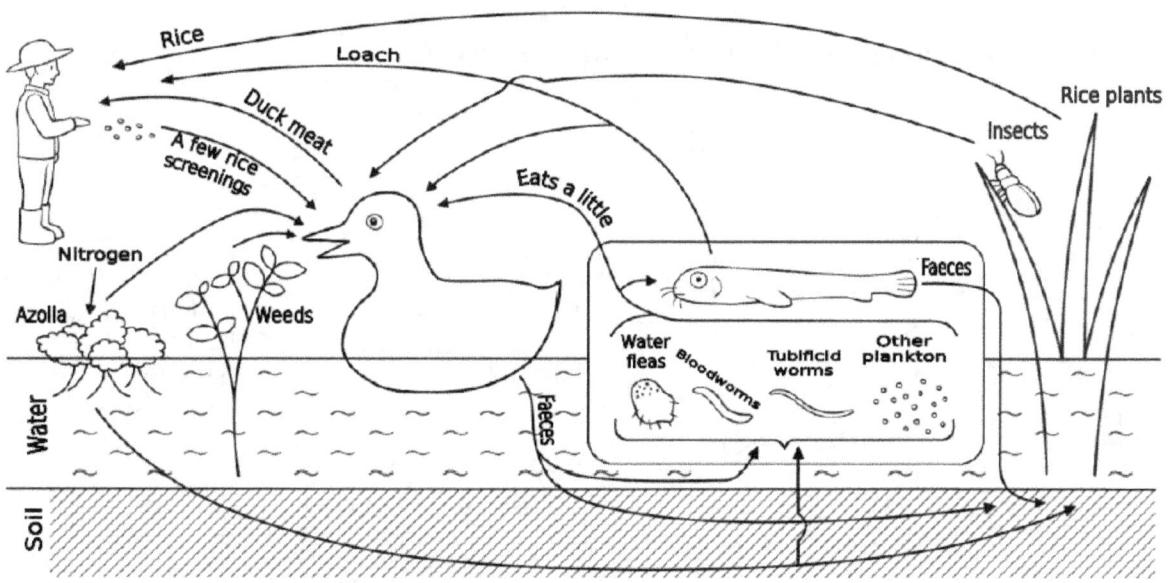

Source: Takao Furuno, IRDF Expanding Toward Infinity, p. 86. [43]

---

[13] See Makino [83], Watanabe [121] or Furuno [66] for more on loaches.
[14] See Katano [15] for more on catfish.

## 2-2-(9) Reintroducing livestock

IRDF also serves to highlight certain fundamental issues in livestock breeding. These days, chickens, pigs and cattle are raised in large numbers in places removed from human habitation. We almost never see livestock in our daily lives.

In the 1960s and earlier, chickens, cows, pigs and goats were kept around people's houses. This is why they are called *kachiku*, literally "house animals," in Japanese. Chickens roamed around people's gardens, and are thus called *niwatori*, literally "garden birds," in Japanese. In other words, human-livestock relations were a part of everyday existence.

"Livestock" no longer exist in this sense in Japan today.

It was under these circumstances that ducks began making an appearance near houses for everyone to see. This is a like a "second advent" of livestock in modern Japan. This is why *aigamo* ducks are enjoying such great popularity.

Livestock are said to have three main functions. There are "production animals" that provide meat, eggs, etc.; "draft or work animals" that pull carts, ploughs, etc.; and "manure animals" which produce fertilizer with their faeces and urine. Modern livestock breeding has focused solely on the first of these, the production animals that give us meat, eggs, and so on.

In IRDF, the ducks swim around freely, performing a new role, "fun work animals," while providing nutrients as "manure animals" and ultimately giving us delicious meat as "production animals."

**Figure 2-10. Diagram of duck abilities realized in IRDF**

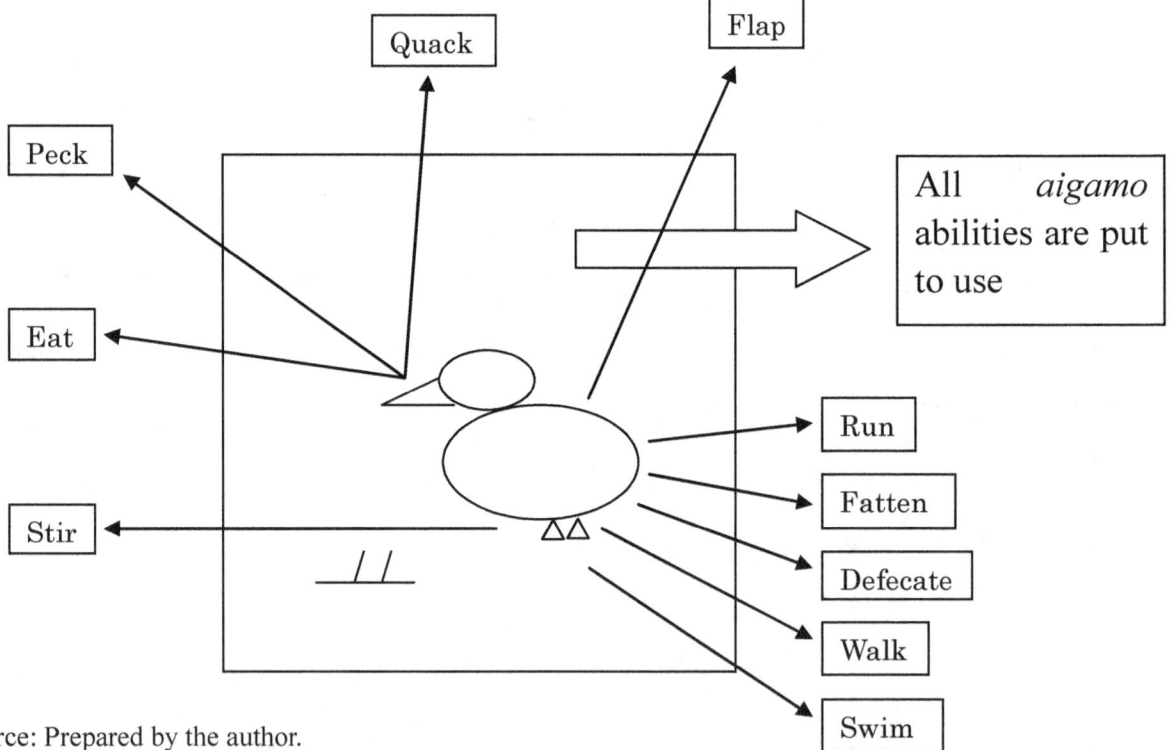

Source: Prepared by the author.

As "work animals," ducks differ from oxen and horses that pull heavy carts or ploughs in the fields under a blazing sun. Ducks move around the broad paddy field freely, at leisure, eating, playing, defecating and sleeping. As a result, the rice plants grow up naturally. Figure 2-10 illustrates the various behaviours of ducks which are realized in a paddy field. The ducks eat, dabble, pull, call, flap their wings, fatten up, provide manure, run, waddle and swim, demonstrating a variety of abilities.

IRDF is a technological system in which all facets of the abilities of ducks (i.e., livestock) are allowed to develop in the paddy fields. For this reason, the ducks in the paddy fields look happy. This is also a livestock welfare-related issue.

## 2-2-(10) Posing the question of the meaning of life

Ducks are livestock. After the rice is harvested at the beginning of winter, they are slaughtered, butchered and eaten. Learning of this, some people complain that it is cruel to kill the poor ducks.

Certainly, killing and eating the ducks that worked all summer in the paddy fields seems barbaric.

In that case, why is it not considered barbaric to buy chicken at the supermarket? The poor chicken! If animals are to continue living, however, they must kill and eat some other living thing. We humans are likewise a link in the chain of life, and we live by taking the lives of other living things.

The problem is that modern humans live in a marketplace economy where labour has become specialized, and this has caused us to lose sight of the fundamentally inter-linked chain of life. Even in IRDF, if farmers are raising large numbers of ducks, they often contract out the job of slaughtering the ducks to someone else. This is specialization of labour. Even so, anybody can see that the ducks floating around the paddy field are alive—they are "livestock."

Life is first appreciated through relationships. The ducks sitting in a nearby paddy field present us with the question of the meaning of life. This is the educational power of ducks as livestock.

## 2-2-(11) Reducing energy consumption — a direction for future development —

IRDF is by no means a perfected technology. I have continued to work on it since 1988, when I first released ducklings into a paddy field.

Table 2-1 and Figure 2-12 are compilations of data that focus on the establishment and development of this technology. As you can see in Table 2-1, I began developing IRDF once I succeeded in protecting my ducks with an electric fence. From there, development proceeded in the direction of expanding the diverse forms of productivity in the paddy fields. I started with rice plants only, added ducks, proceeded to rice + ducks + azolla, and then arrived at rice

+ ducks + azolla + fish.

Since 2003, reduced energy consumption has been my direction in further developing IRDF. This has included combining dry-paddy direct sowing with IRDF to create a system of dry-paddy direct sowing with ducks, leaving the electric fence in place all year, and providing fodder for fattening and manure production. The ducks in the paddy field are given primarily nitrogen-rich fodder (oil meal, fish meal, etc.), which increases the nitrogen content of their faeces, which the ducks in their wanderings spread evenly throughout the paddy field.[15]

In this method, feed and fertilizer are provided in a linked, united fashion, improving the functions of the ducks as both manure animals and work animals.

Throughout the last 19 years of developing my IRDF, not all has been smooth sailing. In fact, I have faced setback after setback; at these times I would think up new tricks and create new techniques for overcoming these various problems.

The biggest crisis I faced was in 2002. For the first time in twelve years, the ducks in my paddy field were attacked for three days in a row by an unknown predator. I studied the footprints and determined that the intruder had been a small animal.

**Figure 2-11. Electric fence F-method**

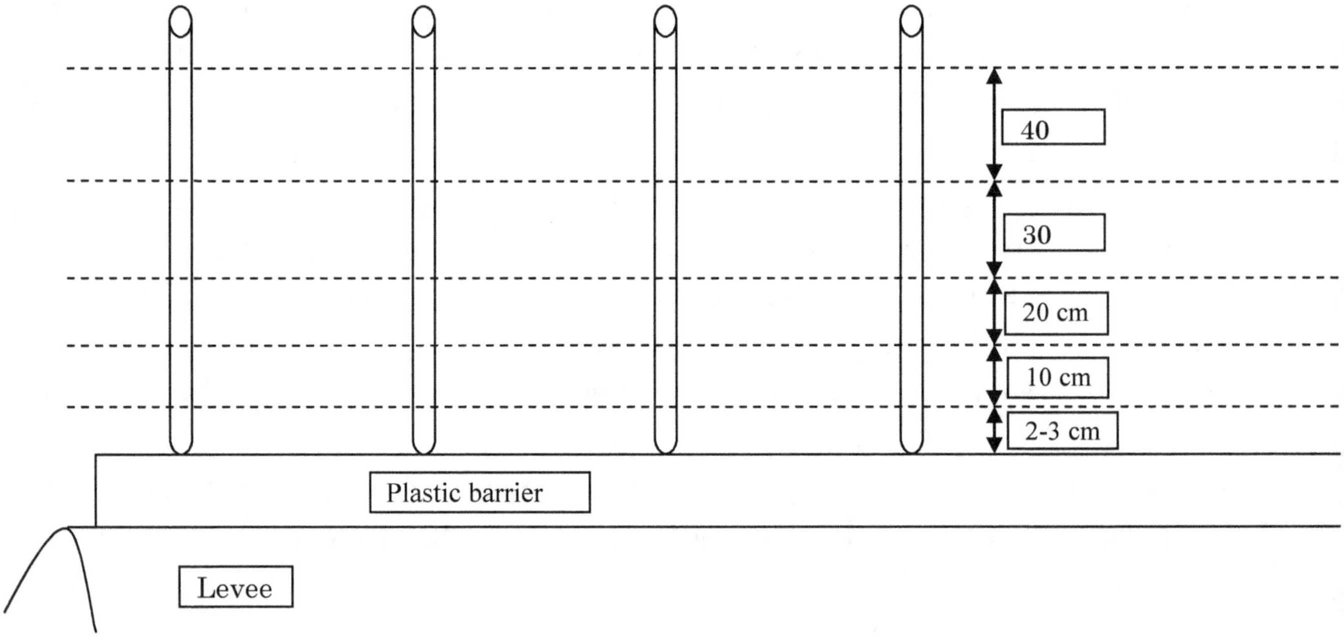

Source: Prepared by the author.

As Figure 2-11 shows, I had not been installing nets around the perimeter of the paddy field, but was using a hard corrugated plastic board 35 cm in height set into the levee with 25 cm of it above ground, and stretching five electric wires above it. I did this in order to have it blend into the scenery and to reduce the amount of labour involved. I called this use of an electric fence without a net the "F-method" ("F" for "Furuno").

---

[15] See Kimoto [21] for more on dry-paddy direct sowing.

My F-method had completely excluded predators for ten years. At first, I thought the small animal had gained entry by going between the electric lines, so I made the spacing between them narrower. This had no effect at all.

Normally the interval between electric shock pulses in electric fences is about one second. I asked the manufacturer to reduce the interval between shocks to 0.5 seconds. That stopped the intrusions flat. It was not changing the spaces between the lines, but rather the interval between shocks that worked. That's how I overcame this crisis. The manufacturer currently sells electric fences with electric pulse intervals of 0.5 or 0.75 seconds.

My IRDF has evolved through matching wits with predators.

For anyone wanting more on electric fences and dry-paddy direct sowing with ducks, I will explain about this in further detail in Chapter 6.

**Figure 2-12. Evolution of IRDF**

| | | | | |
|---|---|---|---|---|
| | | Manual weeding<br>↓<br>Manual weeding machine<br>↓<br>'*Enno*'*, Carp, Tadpole shrimp<br>↓ | | |
| 1988 | **Development of IRDF using the seedling transplantation method** | IRDF<br>↓ | | Net only<br>↓ |
| 1990 | | Bird tillage<br>↓<br>*Aigamo* + azolla<br>↓<br>*Aigamo* + azolla + fish | | Net and electric fence<br>↓<br>Electric fence and corrugated plastic levee barrier sheet<br>↓<br>Pulse of electric fence to 0.5 secs.<br>↓ |
| | | ↓ | **Development of techniques for protection against external predators** | |
| 2002 | **IRDF using the dry-paddy direct sowing method (labour-saving technology)** | IRDF<br>↓ | | Permanent installation of electric fence and corrugated plastic levee barrier sheet<br>↓ |
| 2003 | | Dry-paddy direct sowing<br>↓ | | Development of a weed cutting machine that does not cut the plastic sheet |
| 2004 | | Feed fertilizer** | | |

Notes: * Farming support: Farmers support customers by providing safe and nutritious produce and customers support the farmers not only by buying the produce, but also by visiting the farms and fields to help out with some of the farm work.
** Nitrogen rich fodder is provided to the *aigamo* as feed, later to become fertilizer in the form of droppings.

Source: Prepared by the author.

**Table 2-1. Notes on the evolution of IRDF**

| Period | Development Process | Details |
|---|---|---|
| 1988 | First encounter with *aigamo* ducks | (Feb.) Received a memo on a "duck weeding method" written by Toshio Okita of Toyama Pref. from natural agriculturalist Suemitsu Nomiyama in Fukuoka Pref. That summer, installed netting around a paddy field and first released ducks. Surprised at effectiveness at weed control. |
| 1989 to 1990 | Enclosure technique Battle against dogs | In August, 3 dogs attacked the ducks. Called Mr. Okita. Discouraged to hear, "It's impossible where there are many dogs." Plucked up courage and began battle against dogs.<br><br>At wits end in fight against dogs. A series of defeats. Lonely fretful days. |
| | Began using electric fence | By chance, came upon the idea of using an electric fence to keep out dogs. A victory against the dogs. That put an end to the problem. |
| 1991 1992 | From "duck weeding" to "integrated rice & duck farming" | At this juncture, I set aside a control plot within the paddy field and began studying and documenting the multi-faceted effects of ducks on rice plants (weeding, pest control, nutrient supplying, ploughing & muddying, stimulation, golden snail control). |
| | Survey of effects of ducks with control plot | Based on this data, initiated the theory and practice of the general technology of integrated rice & duck farming.<br><br>Met Professor Masaharu Manda of Kagoshima University in Aya-Cho, Miyazaki Prefecture.<br><br>Began an "*Aigamo Suito Dojisaku*" (Integrated Rice & Duck Farming) series in the journal *Gendai Nogyo* (29 parts). |
| | Held *Aigamo* Summit | Held *Aigamo* Summit in Keisen Town. 300 attended from all over Japan. |
| | Publication | Published book *Aigamo Banzai* through *Nobunkyo* (*Noson Gyoson Bunka Kyokai*; Agricultural, Mountain and Fishing Village Culture Association). |
| | General survey | General survey of the *Aigamo* Project in cooperation with the General Agricultural Testing Centre of Fukuoka Prefecture. |
| 1993 | First encounter with azolla for further diversity | Received instruction on the water plant azolla, which fixes atmospheric nitrogen, from Professor Iwao Watanabe, formerly of Mie University. |
| | Publication of video | Published a video on integrated rice & duck farming (Japanese, Vietnamese and English versions) through *Nobunkyo*. |
| 1994 | More sustainable cycle | Conducted practical research on integrated rice & duck farming with azolla. As a result, integrated rice & duck farming becomes a more sustainable cycle. |
| | Bird tilling | Created bird tilling concept and performed testing to verify it. |
| | Dispatched to Asia | Dispatched by JVC to Vietnam. |
| 1995 | Integrated rice farming found in practice in Asian paddy fields | Discovered possibilities for integrated rice & duck farming in Asia.<br><br>Learned of paddy fields in Vietnam where fish are raised along with rice.<br><br>"*Zoku Aigamo Suito Dojisaku*" (Integrated Rice & Duck Farming, Continued) series published in journal *Gendai Nogyo* (14 parts). |

| | | |
|---|---|---|
| 1996 | Fish added | Released loaches in duck paddy field and commenced practical research on integrated rice & duck farming with azolla and fish. |
| 1997 | Fruit trees also added | Began growing figs on the levies. |
| | Publication | Published book *Mugen ni Hirogaru Aigamo Suito Dojisaku* (Integrated Rice & Duck Farming Expanding toward Infinity) through *Nobunkyo*. |
| | Study of soil nitrogen dynamics in duck paddy field | Had Professor Egashira of Kyushu University Soil Sciences Laboratory conduct a study on soil nitrogen dynamics in a duck paddy field. |
| 1998 | Unified concept of rotational cultivation and integrated rice & duck farming | "*Tanbo Riyo no Hatake Sakujutsu*" (Art of using a rice paddy field for a vegetable field) series carried by *Gendai Nogyo* (9 parts). Concepts of rotational paddy field farming and integrated rice & duck farming unified. |
| 2000 | Recognize importance of "waterfowl culture" Publication | Publication of book *Waga Ie de Tsukuru Aigamo Ryori* (Recipes for duck dishes we make at home) through *Nobunkyo*, jointly authored by Mizuyo Yamane, Chie Deji, Kumiko Furuno, Suzuko Hokanishi, Fumi Manda and Masaharu Manda) |
| 2001 | Publication of English book | Persuaded by Bill Mollison, originator of Permaculture, to publish book *The Power of Duck--IRDF* (Australia, Tagari Publications). "*Zoku Zoku Aigamo Suito Dojisaku*" (3rd Series of Integrated Rice & Duck Farming) published in *Gendai Nogyo* (27 parts). |
| 2002 | Improved electric fence technology for excluding predators | To cope with small predators like weasels, the interval between electric pulses reduced to 0.5 sec, half the standard, in electric fence. |
| 2003 | Energy-saving technology Direct sowing of dry duck paddy fields | With the aim of producing an energy-saving technology, began combining integrated rice & duck farming with direct sowing of dry paddy fields. |
| 2004 | Fodder/fertilizer | Aiming for enhanced fertilization, provided high-nitrogen oil meal and fish meal as fodder for the ducks in the paddy field. |
| 2006 | Leaving electric fence and plastic barrier up all year | Commenced trial leaving the electric fence and plastic sheet barrier in place year round. Introduced weed cutter that does not cut the hard plastic sheet. |
| (Source: Takao Furuno, presentation at 11th *Aigamo* Forum in Hokkaido, Feb. 27, 2001, with additions.) | | |

30

# Chapter 3

## Special Characteristics of Integrated Rice and Duck Farming (IRDF) in Terms of Farming System Theory

Agriculture has developed in characteristic ways in response to the natural and social conditions in different regions. Differences in historical background and the difference between dry, upland farming and wet rice cultivation make a simple comparison impossible between the European agricultural revolution established in the latter half of the 17th century and the spread of IRDF in Asia, but I will attempt a mostly technical comparison from the viewpoint of the rational use of natural forces focusing on farming systems, i.e. intensification of land use. The purpose of this comparison is not to ask which of the two agricultural methodologies is technically superior, but rather to get a clear idea of both their distinctiveness and universality in terms of farming systems from a broader perspective. I hope this will provide a better overall perspective of IRDF, including its merits and demerits.

### 3-1 The Genealogy of Farming System Theory

Let us take a brief look at the farming system theories of Professor Shinbun Kayo, Professor Jiro Iinuma and Professor Iso-o Iwakata.

#### 1) The Farming System Theory of Professor Shinbun Kayo

Professor Shinbun Kayo defines the concept of 'farming system' as an historical category that identifies a transitional stage in the progress towards agricultural modernization. He shows clearly that the two aspects of 'soil fertility regeneration' and 'the prevention and control of weeds' are the main productivity (i.e. technical) motivations promoting a farming system.

Figure 3-1 is Professor Shinbun Kayo's diagrammatical representation of the land use transition in Europe, which developed from the Three Phase Method through the Grain-Grass Method to the Rotational Cultivation Method – the so-called European agricultural revolution. In the final Rotational Cultivation Method phase, the animal feed base was enlarged by introducing red clover and root crops, enclosing the fields with hedgerows, and abolishing the fallowing of land as had been carried out under the Three Phase Method and Grain-Grass Method. As you can see from Figure 3-1, the Rotational Cultivation Method was a four-year rotation in the form of wheat → root crops for animal feed → barley → red clover, in which feed crops were cultivated on three-quarters of the farmland. Livestock were no longer grazed on wild meadows and fallows, as they had been in the Three Phase Method and the Grain-Grass Method, but raised in sheds and given feed crops the year round, the manure generated being returned to the farmland. This was the path of development up to the

Rotational Cultivation Method. In brief, it was an evolution that progressed as follows: increase in feed crops planted → increase in livestock productivity → increase in manure → increase in food crop productivity. This enhancement of soil fertility regeneration was established through the bond between crop and livestock farming.

**Figure 3-1. Land Use Change in the Transition from the Three Phase Method to the Rotational Cultivation Method**

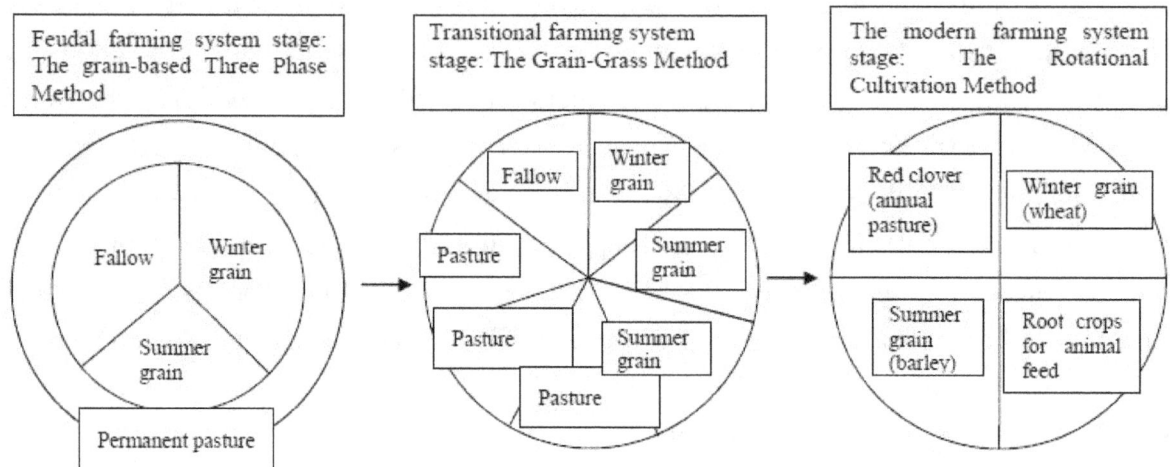

Notes:
1. From a diagram of planting systems by Lujo Brentano, with some additions.
2. The annual order of field planting is indicated by a clockwise rotation.
3. Winter grains (autumn-sown grains) are wheat or rye, summer grains (spring-sown grains) are barley or oats or in some locations include broad beans, garden peas and so on. In the grain and pasture rotation the pasture is mainly perennial Poaceae family grass pasture, including some leguminous pasture of white clover and so on.

Source: Shinbun Kayo, *Japanese Farming System Theory*, 1972, p.8

At the same time, a weed prevention and control system was established through the use of animal power in such techniques as row planting, inter-row weeding, and deep ploughing in the summer for root crops.

For a long while, Japanese agriculture depended on grass and other green manure materials brought in from outside the fields to maintain soil fertility. Grass was cut from meadows or forested hills, carried to the fields by human or animal labour, and put down in the fields together with human wastes. The prevention and control of weeds, symbolized by weeding in paddy fields under a burning sun, was mainly carried out by excruciating human labour. The fusion of crop and livestock farming did not take place in Japan as it had in Europe, and it can be said that dramatic increases in soil productivity and the release of farmers from weeding labour only came with the advent of chemical fertilizers, pesticides, herbicides and machinery introduced with the modernization of agriculture.

The modernization of Japan's agriculture merely substituted chemical fertilizers for the green manure and herbicides for hand weeding, and no farming system revolution matching that of the European agricultural revolution occurred. This is the farming system theory of

Professor Shinbun Kayo.[16]

## 2) The Farming System Theory of Professor Jiro Iinuma

The keynote of Professor Jiro Iinuma's farming system theory is a line drawn between the areas where intertillage, or cultivating between the rows of a crop, was normally carried out (the intertillage zone) and areas where it was not (the non-intertillage zone). At issue here is the idea that there is a fundamental difference in the development process between agricultural methods with and without intertillage. "There is a clear difference in the process of agricultural development between the intertillage zone and the non-intertillage zone. As above, in the intertillage zone the task of intertilling was indispensable and effective, but in the non-intertillage zone it was unnecessary, or was carried out and found to be relatively ineffective. However, this task of intertillage was extremely difficult to carry out whether using livestock or machinery. Thus, whereas agricultural development in the intertillage zone was naturally pushed forward mainly in the direction of strengthening the labour-intensive, intertillage effect, agricultural development in the non-intertillage zone was pushed forward mainly in the direction of strengthening the use of animal power and then on to mechanization…

"The future of agriculture in Japan, being an intertillage zone environment, is thought to differ from the direction of agricultural development in the non-intertillage zone." [3]

## 3) The Farming system Theory of Professor Iso-o Iwakata

The special characteristic of Professor Iso-o Iwakata's farming system theory is his notion of productive power.

"If agricultural labour and the means of production are factors in productive power, the systematic use of labour, the condition of the land over the year, the selection of crops and methods of cultivation, including the labour process necessary to carry these out, are closely intertwined and must coalesce into a single system if productive power is to be realized. From this viewpoint, the term farming system is often used as a generic term for these intertwined forms. If labour is still at a low-level, this must be supplemented by much more finely organizing the labour process; this is also true when intensive management practices need to be maintained. Overall, it is for this reason that traditional Japanese agriculture practice has its own characteristic features, or more specifically, that Japanese agriculture has evolved practices that are intimately linked with each different region and has established complex so-called work systems or customary work practices. Intensification of the labour process is the basis of the modernization of agricultural management, and by making it ever more standardized, even though this may mean standardization of the complex regional customary labour practices, it will still result in even more close-knit interconnectivity between the factors comprising agriculture methods." [7]

---

[16] See Kayo [14] for the farming system theory of Professor Shinbun Kayo.

This is the way Professor Iso-o Iwakata defines "farming system." Furthermore, in his book "Theory of Management with Livestock," he calls Japanese livestock farming "agriculture with livestock." This is distinct from "livestock management farming,"[17] carried out during the European agricultural revolution, which involved livestock production accompanied by feed crop production using a rationalized rotation system. Professor Iso-o Iwakata advocated combining "agriculture with livestock" into a land use system that would result in a characteristically Japanese type of "livestock management farming." This is a very practical farming system theory.

The way in which these three professors, Shinbun Kayo, Jiro Iinuma, and Iso-o Iwakata, comprehend the European agricultural revolution is very similar, but we can see differences in the way they position Japanese agriculture within their farming system theories and the future direction of development.

(This paper referred to Professor Shinbun Kayo for the European agricultural revolution, to the farming system theory of Professor Jiro Iinuma for the theoretical study of natural conditions, and to the farming system theory of Iso-o Iwakata for the theory of productive power.)

## 3-2 A Technical Comparison of the European Agricultural Revolution and IRDF

Table 3-1 is a technical comparison of the European agricultural revolution and IRDF. There are some very interesting resemblances and differences among the so-called planting method, enclosure and livestock raising method, weed control, and soil fertility maintenance methods that cannot be seen in a comparison with modern farming techniques, and which have their basis in the similarities and differences between 'rotational cultivation' and 'integrated/synchronous cultivation.'

### 3-2-(1) Enclosure and the function of livestock

Under the European Three Phase Method, from spring to autumn, small or medium sized livestock such as sheep were put out to graze in common pastures during the day and sheltered in animal sheds near the house at night. Because of the shortage of feed during the winter, many animals were slaughtered before the onset of winter. In the Grain-Grass Method, livestock were grazed on common pasture land or collectively grazed on farmland planted with perennial pasture grass and were kept in sheds overnight.

Under the Rotational Cultivation Method,[18] however, the dispersed farmlands of the Three Phase and Grain-Grass Methods were exchanged and consolidated, and then enclosed and privatized. The common grazing of livestock ended, livestock were raised in sheds and provided with feed all year round. Feed crops were planted on three-quarters of the farmland area, strengthening the feed base. The problem of the lack of winter feed was the main

---

[17] See Iwakata [7] concerning livestock management farming.
[18] See Kayo [14] for details of the rotational cultivation planting method.

bottleneck in the Three Phase and Grain-Grass Methods and this was resolved particularly by the introduction of turnips as livestock feed.

| Table 3-1. A Technical Comparison of the Rotational Cultivation Method in the European Agricultural Revolution and IRDF | | |
|---|---|---|
| | Rotational Cultivation Methodology brought about by the European Agricultural Revolution | Integrated Production Methodology brought about by IRDF |
| **Enclosure and livestock raising method** | ● Enclosure: Privatization of farms through the exchange and consolidation of dispersed farmland and enclosure of fields.<br>● Raising of livestock in sheds instead of grazing on farmland or pasture.<br>● Enclosure of livestock in sheds.<br>● Year-round provision of feed crops. | ● Enclose the paddy field with a fence, and allow the waterfowl (domesticated ducks) to graze directly among the standing rice plants in the paddy field. (Traditional duck paddy field grazing allowed ducks to freely graze in unenclosed paddy fields.)<br>● Enclosure of grain (rice) and livestock (*aigamo*) together. |
| **Planting method** | ● Four-year rotation of winter grain (wheat) → root crop (feed crop) → summer grain (barley) → red clover (annual pasture grass)<br>● Elimination of fallows<br>● Elimination of common grazing lands | ● Integrated production of rice, duck, azolla (feed crop) and fish.<br>● Rice and ducks only in the beginning.<br>● At present rice, azolla, ducks and fish (loach). |
| **Weed prevention and control** | ● Innovation in labour methods<br>● Sowing of seeds by animal-powered row planter, inter-row removal of weeds by animal-powered inter-row weeding machines.<br>● Removal of roots of weedy perennials through deep ploughing before sowing of root crops.<br>● Labour-intensive technique (since people use livestock to carry out tasks) | ● Animal-powered inter-row weeding by ducks.<br>● Creative use of energy from animal power.<br>● Ducks perform both inter-row and inter-hill weeding (weeding between rice hills).<br>● Object of labour (livestock) becomes the means of labour<br>● Labour-saving technique (since the livestock carry out the task) |
| **Soil fertility maintenance** | ● Introduction of annual pasture grass and root crop (e.g. beets).<br>● Expansion of planted area, expansion of feed crop area → increase of number of livestock raised in sheds→ increase in amount of manure→ increased productivity.<br>● Unlike grazing, harvesting of feed crops, provision of feed to livestock, carrying and spreading of manure from livestock sheds to farmland, etc. require intensive labour. | ● Ducks eat feed, weeds, insect pests, aquatic animals and so on and their faeces provide nutrients for the rice plants.<br>● Nitrogen-fixing azolla cultivated between the standing rice plants is used as a feed crop.<br>● Labour saving, since rice and livestock are produced simultaneously in the enclosed paddy field, eliminating the need to carry and spread manure. |

Source: Prepared by the author based on *Japanese Farming System Theory* by Shinbun Kayo. [14]

Looking at the European agricultural revolution from the viewpoint of farming system theory with a focus on enclosure and livestock in this way, we can see that productivity was expanded when the common grazing of livestock generally carried out under the Three Phase and Grain-Grass Methods was transformed under the Rotational Cultivation Method to grazing livestock in enclosed, privately-owned farmland and altering the enclosure method of livestock to sheds. As mentioned above, livestock play various roles in the relationship between crop farming and livestock farming - as draught or work animals, as production animals (for food and other animal products), and as providers of manure. The draught and manure functions were the most important in the Three Phase and Grain-Grass Methods, but under the Rotational Cultivation Method, their role as production animals and providers of manure were particularly reinforced due to the increased number of animals that could be raised in sheds. They also played an important draught animal role in row planting, deep ploughing, and so on.

Changes in the type of labour used in the European agricultural revolution meant that labour was mainly performed by large livestock such as cattle and horses. The livestock that perform the work in IRDF are the small to medium sized *aigamo* ducks, which perform their relaxed role directly.

As I will mention in more detail in Chapter 4, in traditional duck paddy field grazing generally carried out in Asian countries, ducks were allowed to graze in paddy fields during the daytime after rice seedlings had been transplanted into the paddies. There were no fences around any of the paddy fields and the ducks were allowed to move freely from one paddy field to another. The ducks were kept in sheds near the house at night. We can say that this 'common duck grazing' system is analogous to the common grazing of the European Three Phase and Grain-Grass Methods.

In IRDF, however, as with the enclosures of the Rotational Cultivation Method, a fence is set up around the paddy field and the *aigamo* ducks and the standing rice plants are enclosed together. In traditional duck paddy field grazing, the ducks are the most important as production animals, but in IRDF all the functions – the draught animal function, the production animal function, and the manure function – are important.

Nevertheless, the draught animal function in the Rotational Cultivation Method agricultural practice differs in form from that in IRDF. In the former, not all the livestock are used as draught animals, only the working animals that pull the intertillage machine or the plough. In the latter, however, all the livestock are draught animals, production animals and manure animals all the time. Furthermore, as mentioned in Chapter 2, these are freely working 'take-it-easy livestock.'

In short, from the point of view of enclosure and livestock functions, as seen in Figure 3-2, farmland and livestock were enclosed separately in the European agricultural revolution, but in IRDF, as seen in Figure 3-3, the standing grain and the *aigamo* ducks are enclosed together on the farmland. These agricultural methodologies are the same in that they both enclose livestock and farmland, but a closer examination shows that in the European system the livestock were linked to *rotations* and in the Japanese integrated farming the livestock are technically distinct in a very interesting way.

The European agricultural revolution was carried out in an upland farming environment and IRDF is wet rice cultivation, so naturally the outcomes are different. However, the issue I would like to raise has to do with the production system technique.

In the Rotational Cultivation Method, wheat, feed root crops, barley, red clover and so on are rotated 'diachronically' (in succession), and the livestock are raised in sheds by providing them with the feed crops.

**Figure 3-2. The European Agricultural Revolution Enclosure**

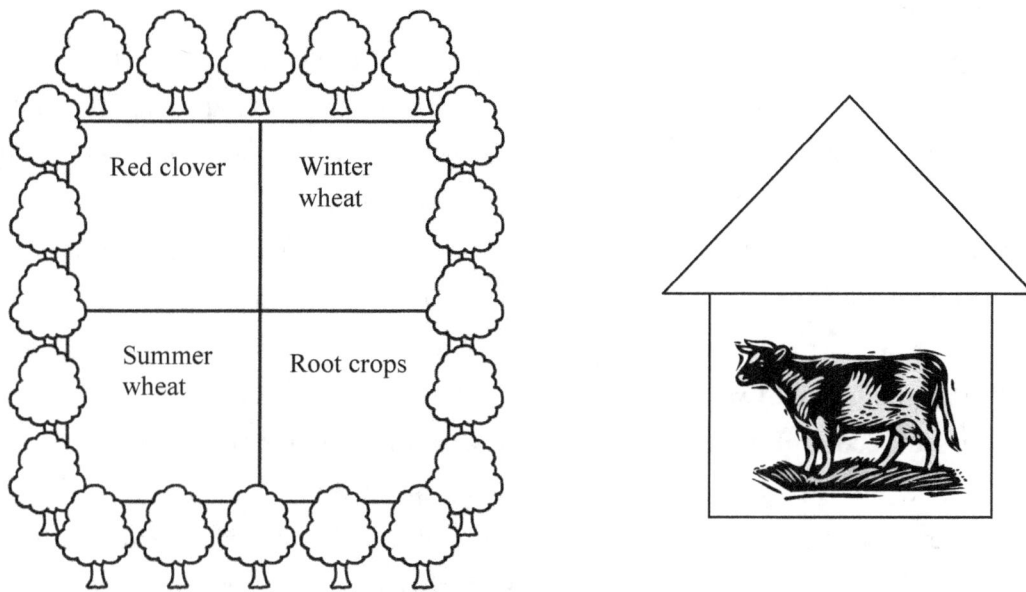

Farmland enclosed by hedgerows                    Livestock kept in sheds

Source: Prepared by the author

**Figure 3-3. The IRDF Enclosure**

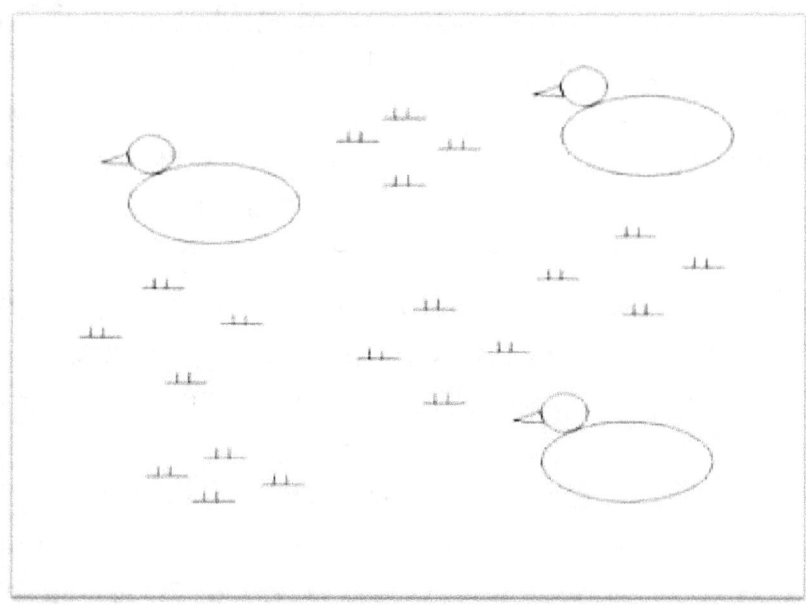

Source: Prepared by the author.

### 3-2-(2) The so-called 'Planting Method'

In IRDF, rice, azolla (a nitrogen-fixing aquatic fern), livestock and fish are raised 'synchronically' (simultaneously) in the same space. This is the fundamental difference in the two production system techniques. Planting usually means that 'crops' are planted in fields and the 'planting method' mainly refers to the order in which crops are planted. It is uncertain whether the term 'planting method' is appropriate for the IRDF method, in which rice, azolla, *aigamo* ducks and fish are produced simultaneously, but here I would like to consider this as a corresponding concept.

Looking at the production of feed crops in terms of quantity, in the Rotational Cultivation Method, ample feed crops are produced on three-quarters of the farmland area. In IRDF, weeds, insect pests and aquatic animals as well as nitrogen fixing azolla are amply produced as feed crops (green feed) between the rice plants in the paddy field.

These are the differences and similarities in the so-called planting method between the 'rotations' of the Rotational Cultivation Method and the 'synchronic' cultivation of IRDF.

### 3-2-(3) Prevention and control of weeds

Weed prevention and control in the European agricultural revolution was established through innovations in the mechanical means of labour; the invention of the deep tillage plough, animal-powered seed sowing machinery, and animal-powered intertillage machinery. In other words, deep ploughing was carried to cultivate root crops for feed, seed formerly broadcast sown was now sown in equidistant rows, and inter-row weeding was carried out between the crop rows by animal-powered intertillage machine. As in the European agricultural revolution, IRDF also uses 'animal-powered inter-row weeding' by simply placing the source of the animal power (*aigamo* ducks) directly into the field. As well as being a means of labour, the *aigamo* ducks are at the same time the object of labour. When people feed the *aigamo* ducks in the paddy field the ducks are the object of labour, and when they eat the weeds and insect pests they are the means of labour. In IRDF, the rice and the ducks grow together. The growing ducks become able to stretch out their necks to reach the insects high up on the leaves of the rice plant. We can say that this is, in contrast to mechanical means of labour, 'a means of labour that grows.'

In the Rotational Cultivation Method, people use oxen and horses to plant crop seeds in rows with an animal-powered row-planting machine as seen in Figure 3-4, and subsequently carried out inter-row weeding between the rows of the crop using an animal-powered intertillage machine, as seen in Figure 3-5, pulled by oxen or horses.

In IRDF, rather than people using ducks to carry out inter-row weeding, the ducks carry out animal-powered intertillage continuously and of their own free will as they grow. Furthermore, they carry out intertillage between the rice plants making no distinction between inter-row and inter-hill weeding. In addition, in principle, the *aigamo* duck, a small to medium sized livestock animal, is capable of carrying out inter-row weeding (intertillage) in not only cases in which seedlings are transplanted, but also in cases of direct sowing, spot sowing or row sowing. The animal-powered inter-row weeding of the Rotational Cultivation Method requires the precondition of row sowing by an animal-powered row sowing machine, whereas IRDF does not necessarily require this precondition. In this sense it can be said that IRDF is a creative use of animal power.

The weed prevention and control techniques[19] of the European agricultural revolution are said to have been established through innovations in the mechanical means of labour, but what innovations can we say led to the weed prevention and control technique established in IRDF? It was achieved through the enclosure of *aigamo* ducks in the paddy field. This enclosure corresponds to the 'container-like means of labour' that is mentioned in Professor Iso-o Iwakata's *Introduction to Agricultural Management*.[20] I will go more deeply into this point in Chapter 6. This completes the section on the technical differences between the two agricultural methodologies from the point of view of weed prevention and control.

### 3-2-(4) Maintenance of soil fertility

In the European agricultural revolution, a system of improved soil fertility regeneration (expansion of production of feed crops → increase in the number of shed-raised livestock → increased productivity) was established within the farmland. In general, this kind of system of improved soil fertility regeneration based on crop rotations has not yet been realized in IRDF. Nevertheless, because in IRDF the rice crop and the livestock occupy the same space at the same time, the rice screenings provided as feed, the weeds, the insect pests, the aquatic animals and the azolla eaten by the ducks become excreta, which then can be directly used by the rice plants as nutrients. In addition, in contrast to closed-off upland field production, various kinds of nutrients flow into the paddy field with the irrigation water.

Thus, in IRDF, the rice crop, the livestock production and the cultivation and provision of the feed crop (azolla as a green feed) all occur simultaneously in the same space. This is different from European agricultural revolution system, where upland field production and livestock production are carried out in separate locations, are then linked together at the animal shed, from where the animal excreta are returned to the field, thereby forming a cycle with the feed crops and the fertilizer (composted manure).

As in Figure 3-6, the European Rotational Cultivation Method is an advanced land use system, but normally requires intensive labour for such tasks as harvesting feed crops, provision of feed to the livestock, and carrying and spreading of compost. This intensive labour is not required in the case of livestock grazing under the Three Phase Method or the grain and pasture system. However, land use under these systems is much more extensive. This is the technical comparison seen from the point of view of soil fertility maintenance.[21]

---

[19] See Iinuma [3], Iwakata [7], and Kayo [14] concerning the weed prevention and control of the European agricultural revolution.

[20] See Kayo [14] concerning the container-like means of labour.

[21] See Kayo [14] and Watanabe [127] for more detail on the soil fertility maintenance of the European agricultural revolution.

**Figure 3-4. Animal-powered row sowing machine**

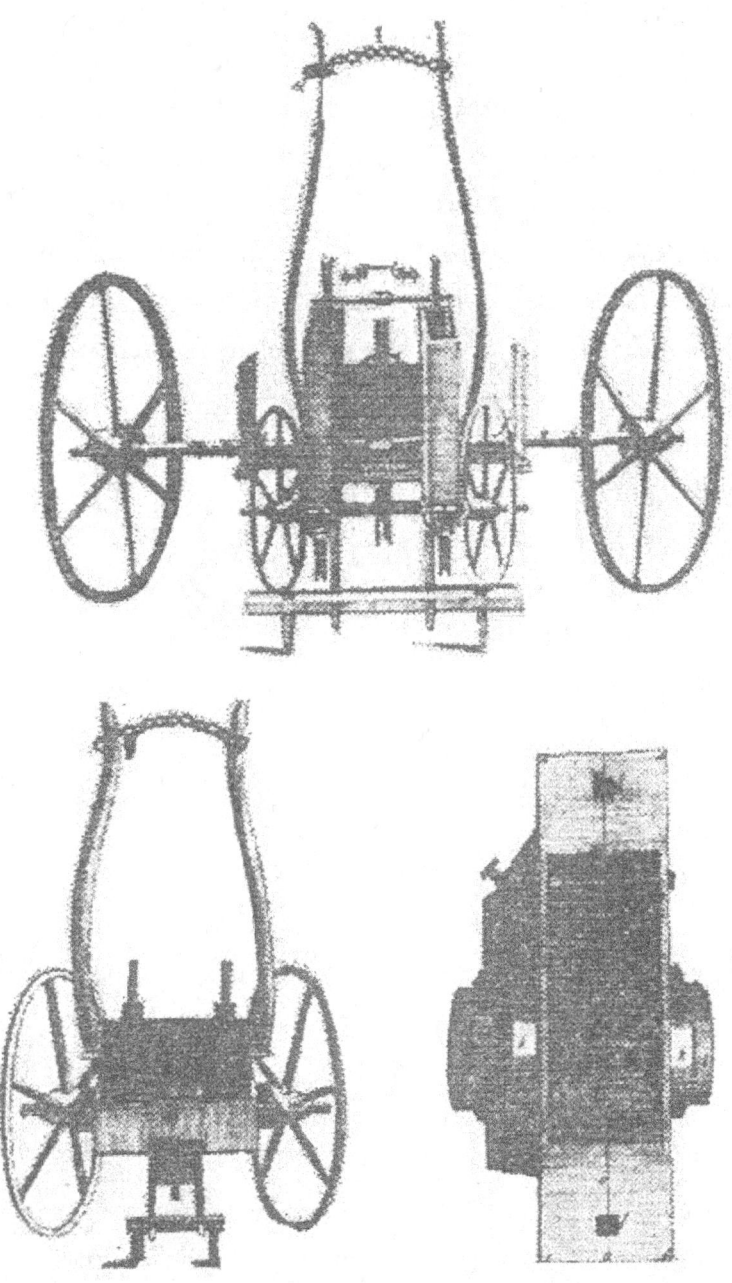

Source: Iinuma, Jiro, *On the Agricultural Revolution*, p.87. [3]

**Figure 3-5. Animal-powered intertillage machine (intertiller, row tiller)**

Source: Iinuma, Jiro, *On the Agricultural Revolution*, p.89. [3]

**Figure 3-6. Material circulation between farmland and animal sheds in rotational cultivation**

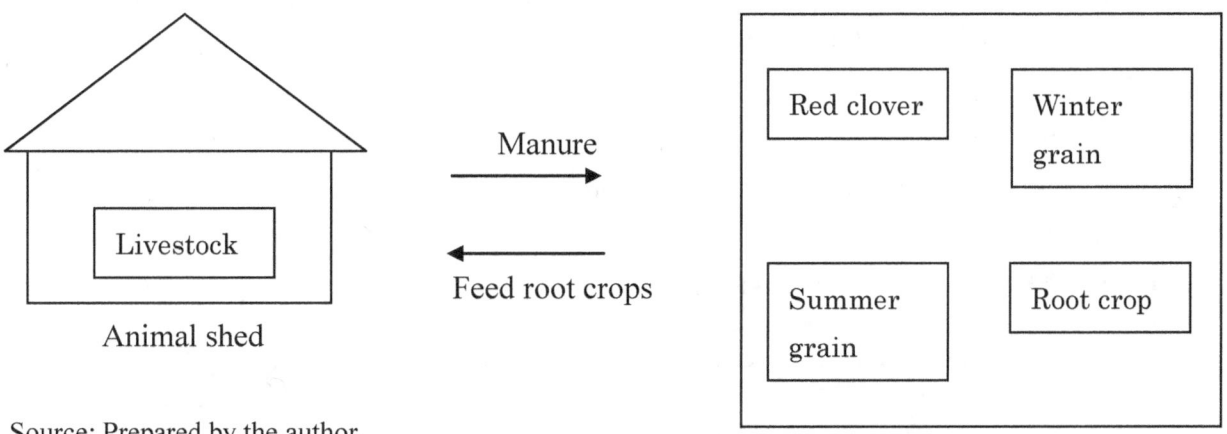

Source: Prepared by the author.

### 3-2-(5) Summary

The European agricultural revolution was established on the basis of the development of advanced animal-powered ploughing techniques, for example deep ploughing in preparation for sowing feed root crops. As long as we take this as the model, animal power will probably mean 'large livestock.' This is because the development of ploughing cultivation systems is difficult with 'small- and medium-sized livestock.'

The *aigamo* duck is small-sized livestock, but swimming backwards and forwards around a water-filled paddy field it grows to maturity while providing the *aigamo* duck effects of weed prevention and control, nutrient provision, stimulation, muddying, golden snail suppression and control that benefit the rice without harming the rice plants. This would not be possible in a system of large-sized livestock and mechanical means of labour in a water-filled paddy field.

"If the modernization of Japanese agriculture can only be thought of as following in the direction of Westernization, then the future of Japanese agriculture is dark indeed. However, with conditions prevailing in Japan that are not present in the West, which are moreover conditions that constitute strong obstacles to the Westernization of Japanese agriculture, if it is possible to think of the 'modernization' of Japanese agriculture in a direction that, on the contrary, makes use of these conditions, then the future of Japanese agriculture will look a lot brighter." [3]

IRDF, which is an organic fusion of the living creatures of the Asian paddy field, the wet rice, waterfowl, aquatic plants, and paddy field fish, is then a direction that makes use of the characteristics of water and paddy fields that Professor Jiro Iinuma suggests are strong obstacles to the Westernization of Asian agriculture.

In brief, it can be said that IRDF is a technological system that (as in Figure 3-7) makes use of the labour-saving nature of grazing as in the Three Phase and Grain-Grass Methods and simultaneously incorporates weed prevention/control and soil fertility maintenance as seen in the Rotational Cultivation Method in the form of an integrated farming technique. However, in its usual form, the IRDF system of soil fertility improvement and regeneration does not include a system that corresponds to that carried out through 'crop rotation' in the European agricultural revolution. Crop rotation combined with integrated farming, as I am practicing now, is a future issue for IRDF, as I shall mention in the next section.

I think the above has clarified the uniqueness and universality of IRDF through a comparison with the European agricultural revolution.

**Figure 3-7. Material recycling in IRDF**

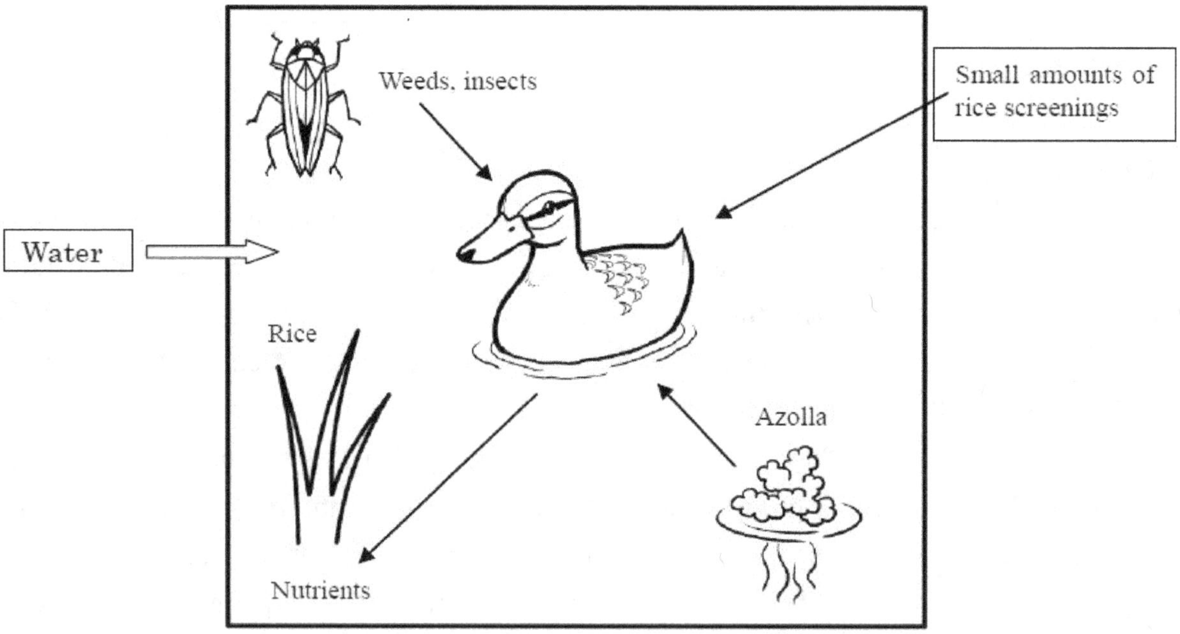

Source: Prepared by the author.

## 3-3 A Comparison of Asian Agricultural Development and IRDF

How can we position IRDF within traditional Asian agriculture? Tadayo Watanabe has discussed the direction of Asian agricultural development in the following way:

"The background to Asian agriculture, especially that of East Asia, is described as farming unaccompanied by livestock, in contrast to the farming accompanied by livestock of Europe. In this context it is necessary to understand that while the latter placed its emphasis on raising livestock and developed its agriculture in the direction of actively introducing the cultivation of feed crops onto the farmland, the latter, Asian agriculture, developed in a different direction, and thus there was a fundamental difference in the developmental path of agriculture between the two.

"What, then, was the direction of the development of agriculture in Asia? As seen in the examples given thus far, the basic strategy was one of cultivating as large a variety of food crops as possible throughout the year, and endeavouring to maximize productivity per unit area for the total of all crop varieties rather than trying to maximize the yields of single crops. The planting methods such as East Asian multiple cropping in paddy fields and the mixed cropping and intercropping of Indian upland agriculture, and the thoroughgoing cultivation management techniques that supported these methods, are straightforward examples that indicate this agricultural development path." [127]

I am sure this is correct. Up until the 1950s, the agriculture in the village where I live was also bustling with activity. We had not yet completed the paddy field reform at that time, so the paddy fields were all shapes and sizes, and there were persimmon, cape jasmine and willow trees planted here and there on the paddy field levees. Multiple cropping of the paddy fields was carried out, with the paddy fields filled with rapeseed, Chinese milk vetch and winter grains in the spring, and rice in the summer with soybeans or *azuki* beans on the levees. In the autumn we caught river fish in the irrigation canals and ponds, and in the winter we went up into the slopes behind the house to gather firewood. In the upland fields, a great variety of vegetables were cultivated. We kept livestock such as cattle, horses, goats and chickens. In short, this was the type of farming where all families produced all kinds of crops for their own consumption and sold what excess they had.

The rural scenery of the Red River Delta area of Vietnam when I visited in the autumn of 1994 made a great impression on me. In the paddy fields that had all been planted with rice in the spring, maize, sweet potatoes, peanuts and all kinds and varieties of vegetables were now being cultivated as far as the eye could see and every member of every family was out working in the fields. According to JVC Hanoi, who carried out a survey for me, the multiple cropping of paddy fields is a type of agriculture that has been carried out in the Red River Delta area for a very long time.

If we place IRDF within the genealogy of the developmental direction of traditional Asian agriculture, its significance can be very distinctly understood.

Figure 3-8 shows the recycling structure of organic farming on Furuno Farm.

Figure 3-8. Recycling Structure of the Organic Farming on the Furuno Farm

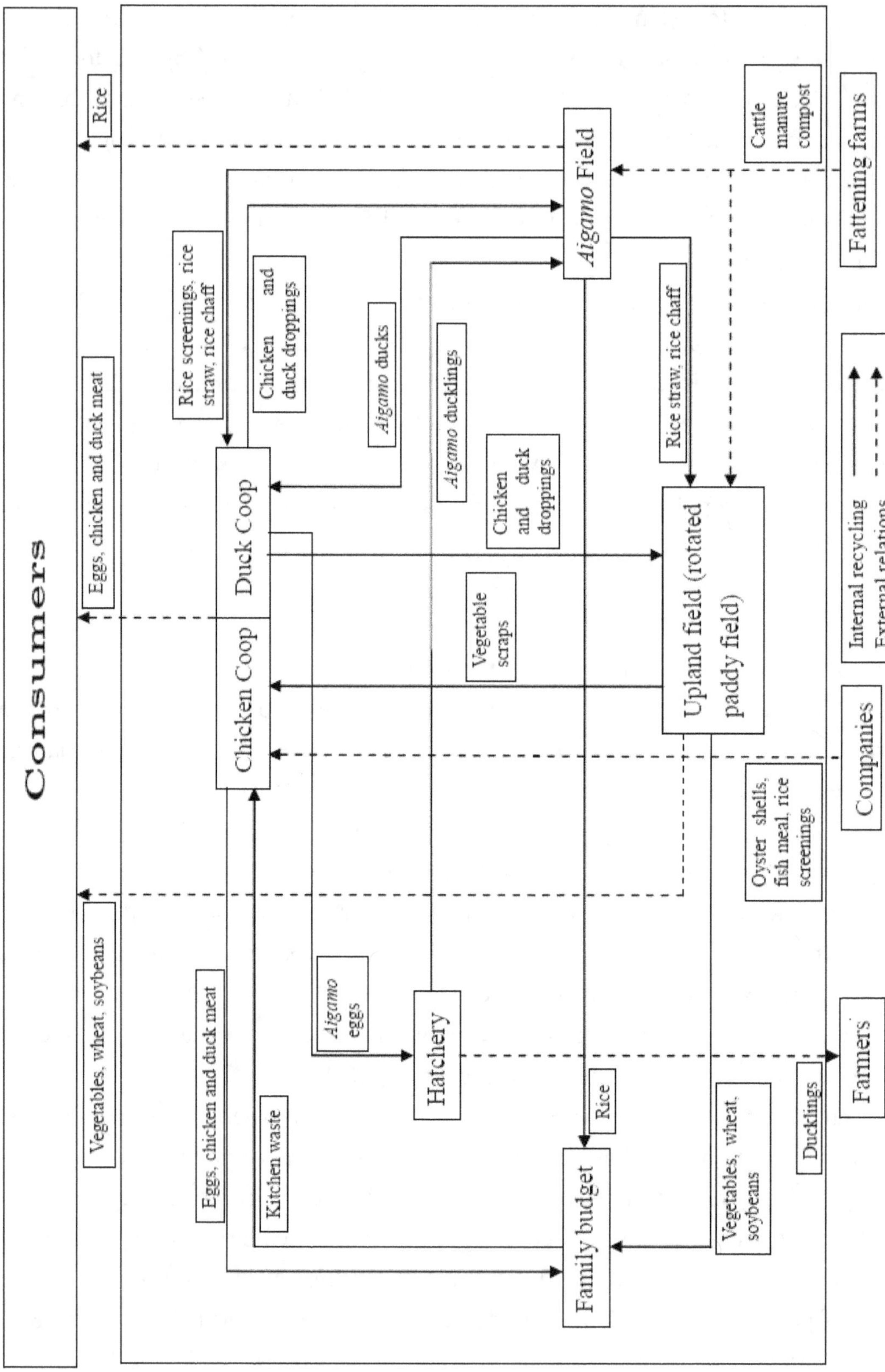

Source: Prepared by the author as material for the 16th National Aigamo Forum, 2006.

Of the 5.4 ha of paddy field I have, I carry out IRDF on 3.4 hectares, cultivate vegetables on 1 ha of rotated paddy field land, and 1 ha of paddy field is set aside. Thus in any one year, roughly one-third of the total paddy field area of the Furuno Farm consists of upland fields on which vegetables are grown organically for three years. After three years, the upland fields are returned to paddy on which IRDF is carried out. An off-season crop is planted in the paddy fields in the winter. After harvesting the rice each year, a crop such as wheat, onions, potatoes, and so on is cultivated in the period before the rice transplanting season the following year.

Paddy fields are always paddy fields, of course, but we can consider them as paddy fields when they have water in them and upland fields when they are dry. This viewpoint sees rice cultivation and upland field cultivation in a continuous and unified way, and this is the way that paddy fields were originally cultivated in the past.

Figure 3-9 is an integrated model of crop rotations and integrated farming. The direction of the vertical arrow indicates crop rotations. Various crops are grown in a 'diachronic' rotation, such as vegetables → rice → wheat, as the seasons change. This kind of crop rotation is a traditional technique that has been widely used in Asian countries, including Japan. In general, when a large variety of crops are grown in rotation, a year-round detailed and thoroughgoing cultivation management scheme is necessary. For example, if a variety of vegetables are grown in a paddy field in a rotation, you end up with inter-row weeding being carried out by hand. Thus, in general, Asian crop rotations are premised on large inputs of human labour.

The direction of the horizontal arrow in Figure 3-9 indicates integrated farming. Rice, *aigamo* ducks, azolla and fish are all cultivated in a 'synchronic and mutually beneficial' manner in the paddy fields in the summer. There are surprisingly few examples of techniques approximating integrated (synchronic) farming methods in traditional Asian agriculture. We can say that the cultivation of fish in paddy fields, which has been widely carried out in Asia for a very long time, is a kind of integrated farming. Examples of this are 'fish-raising in paddy fields' in China, 'carp-raising in paddy fields' in Japan and rice-fish intercropping known as '*minapadi*' in Indonesia. "The Chinese technique of 'fish-raising in paddy fields' has a history of over 2,000 years, but with improvements in agricultural production technology and the modernization of society, the number of paddy fields where fish-raising is carried out has gradually declined. In the northern part of Jiangsu Province, the area of paddy fields under the 'fish-raising in paddy field' regime was 200,000 *mu* (13,200 ha) in 2001, but now only about 10,000 *mu* (660 ha) remain." [137]

However, the degree of tightness of the organic relationship between fish-raising and rice cultivation in this system is uncertain. Is the Chinese 'fish-raising in paddy fields' really an integrated 'rice and fish collaboration?' It is certainly 'synchronic cultivation' because the rice and the fish are being raised together. However, is there not a subtle difference in the organic relatedness between the rice and the fish and the rice and the *aigamo* ducks? The answer is that the fish are active only in the water, whereas the *aigamo* ducks work both on the land and in the water. In the Mekong delta in Vietnam, I have heard that when insect pests appear on the rice, the water is drained from the paddy field, fish being raised in the paddy field are moved and the rice crop is sprayed with chemical insecticides.

**Figure 3-9. An Integration of Crop Rotations and Integrated Farming**

```
                    ┌──────────────┐
                    │              │
                    │  Vegetables  │
                    │              │              (Upland field) 3-year
                    │              │- - - - - - - paddy-upland rotation
Crop                │              │
rotations           │              │
(diachronic)        │              │
         ┌──────────┼──────────┬───┼───────┐
         │          │          │           │  (Paddy        field)
         │ Azolla,  │   Rice   │  Aigamo   │- - Integrated  farming
         │  fish    │          │  ducks    │    in summer
         └──────────┼──────────┴───┼───────┘
                    │              │         (Upland        field)
                    │    Wheat     │- - - - -Off-season crop of
                    │              │         wheat,      onions,
                    │              │         potatoes in winter
                    └──────────────┘
                                                              ──────►
              Integrated farming (synchronic)
```

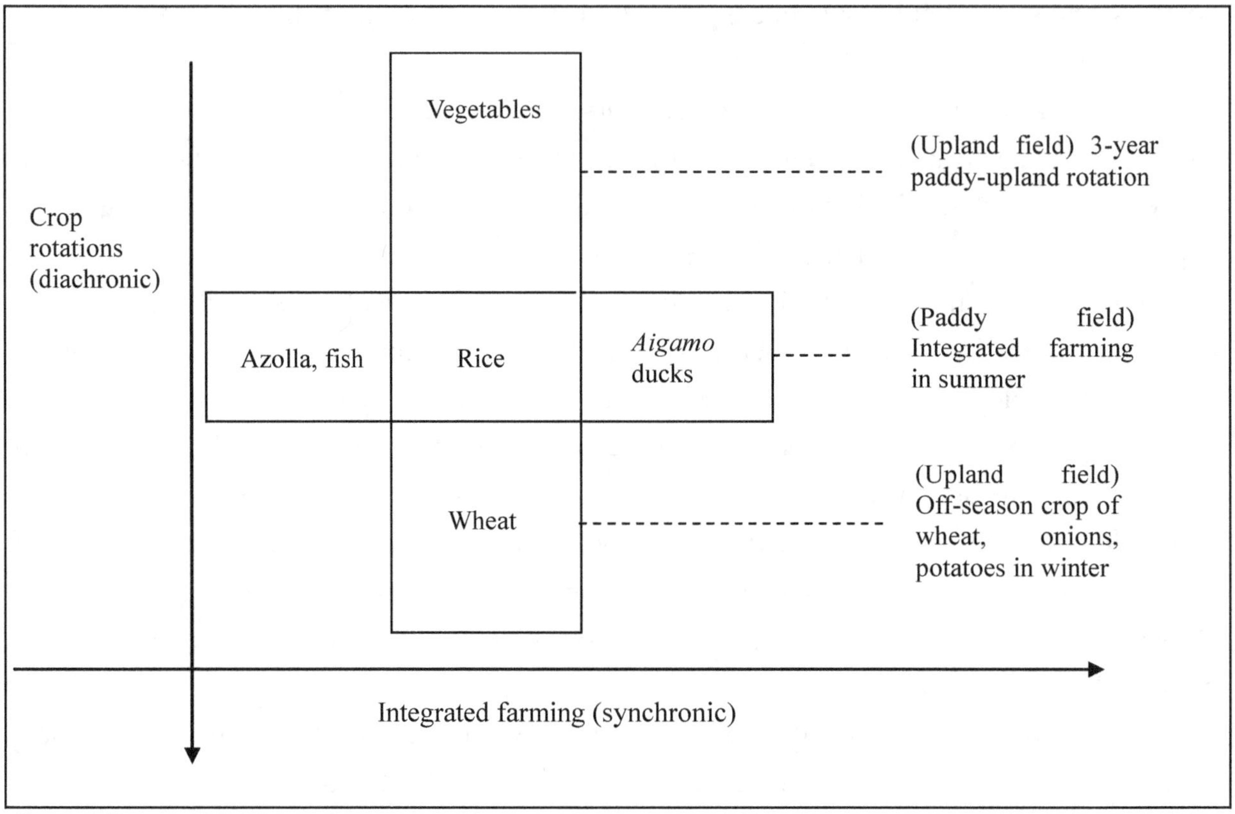

Source: Prepared by the author

With the spread of IRDF across Asia in recent years, the idea of integrated farming has begun to come to the attention of people once again. Images of crop rotations and integrated farming graphically represented in a unified way, as in Figure 3-9, relay a deeper understanding of both methods. This is, as Professor Tadayo Watanabe says, "Making good use of a limited land area both temporally and spatially, and raising the total, overall productive power rather than the productivity of individual crops." [127] Year after year, in the same paddy field and during the same seasonal period, the same crop, rice, is grown repeatedly. The characteristic nature of integrated farming is that the monoculture method for rice is enclosed in order to carry out the synchronous and mutually beneficial cultivation of rice, ducks, azolla and fish. Further, as in Figure 3-9, integrating 'crop rotations' and 'integrated (synchronic) farming' results in a dramatic enrichment of productive power.

Professor Tadayo Watanabe has explained the intercropping and mixed cropping of southern India, shown in Figure 3-10, as follows: "Spatial intensification in the present context is so-called intercropping and mixed cropping in which several different crops are

46

cultivated on the same land at the same time. In other words, this is a planting method under which grains and other crops such as pulses and so on are cultivated together. This method of cultivation makes it possible to harvest more than one crop from one piece of land. Through the beneficial spatial arrangement of a number of crops, it is possible to achieve the same function as carrying out multiple cropping (single crops planted in succession) during a single period of cultivation with several crops planted at the same time. Since crops with different nutrient demands, different growth periods or different growth characteristics are combined when planning the crop combinations, various kinds of effects are brought about. These are, for example, a soil fertility maintenance effect from the nutrient supplementation by the pulses, a soil erosion alleviating effect, an insect pest and weed suppression effect, and so on." [127]

**Figure 3-10. Examples of Mixed Cropping in Southern India**

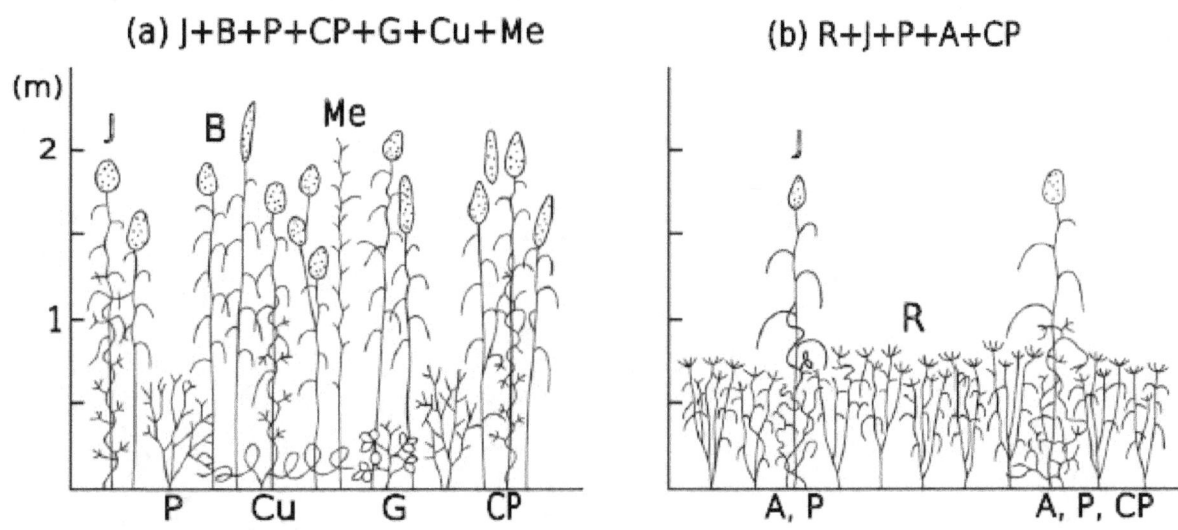

Notes: R: Ragee (*Eleusine coracana*), J: Indian millet/sorghum, B: A pearl millet (*Pennisetum glaucum*), P: Pigeon pea (*Cajanus cajan*), A: Lablab (*Dolichos lablab*), CP: Cow-pea (*Vigna unguiculata*), G: Mung bean, Cu: Melon, Me: Kenaf

Source: Watanabe, Tadayo, *The Era for Considering Agriculture*, p.144. [127]

Intercropping and mixed cropping are forms of 'integrated (synchronous) farming' using the relations between different crop plants. However, when carrying out intercropping and mixed cropping, for example, cultivation management functions such as weeding and so on are almost totally carried out by human labour, requiring larger and more complex labour inputs. Asian agriculture in recent years has seen the introduction of the use of chemical fertilizers and pesticides together with the modernization of agriculture, and the direction of agriculture is moving away from crop rotation, mixed cropping and intercropping traditions towards increased monoculture. In contrast, it is also true that varieties of rice with shorter growing periods were introduced during the 'Green Revolution,'[22] enhancing the ability to carry out multiple cropping.

Our present age is one in which the distinctive coexistence of 'diversity' and 'energy/labour-saving' in IRDF really commands attention. As we have seen from the above, it can be said that IRDF is an integrated technological system that expresses both the 'labour-saving nature' of the animal-powered European agricultural revolution and the diversity of traditional Asian agriculture.[23] In short, IRDF represents a labour-saving direction for agriculture that seeks to enhance land productivity.

---

[22] See Tsuji [30] for the relation between the green revolution and the modernization of agriculture in Asia.
[23] See Guo [129] for details of traditional Chinese agriculture.

# Chapter 4

## Traditional Asian Duck Paddy Field Grazing

If you visit Asia's rice-growing regions, you may encounter the sight of ducks playing in the paddy fields. The methods of raising ducks in rice fields differ considerably among countries and regions. Generally, though, what most traditional Asian methods of raising ducks in paddy fields have in common is that a suitable quantity of ducks are allowed to roam in unenclosed paddy fields by day and then led back home in the evening.

In this chapter I present my observations on the nature of traditional Asian duck paddy field grazing (also known as free-range duck farming systems) based on surveys I have conducted and literature at hand. My objective here is to define integrated rice and duck farming (IRDF) within the scope of the set of traditions known as "Asian waterfowl culture."

### 4-1 Traditional Chinese Duck Paddy Field Grazing

I visited China for the first time in 1992. Since then I have had several opportunities to visit again, with invitations from rice-growing regions in Guangdong, Jiangsu, Anhui, Hunan and Heilongjiang Provinces and the Xinjiang Uyghur and Guangxi Zhuang Autonomous Regions to introduce the concept of IRDF and establish exchanges with duck farmers, who themselves interact with other farmers and authorities. This exchange is still ongoing.

In 1992, I had a chance to observe traditional duck paddy field grazing in Xing'an County, Guangxi Zhuang Autonomous Region. That was the first and last time for me to see that practice. In the fifteen years since, I have visited China on numerous occasions, but have never had a second chance to see traditional duck paddy field grazing in that great land of China, famous for its ducks.

### 4-1-(1) Raising ducks for locust control

The following is an excerpt from *Ancient Agricultural History of China*, edited by the Agricultural History Research Department of the China Agricultural Museum.

"Raising ducks to control locusts was a great invention of the Ming Dynasty (1368-1644) and one of the techniques of biological control. This method of controlling insects is listed in the *Zhihuang Biji* (Notes on Locust Control) written by Chen Jinglun (recorded in the *Zhihuang Jizhuan Xilü*, Locust-Control Annals, of Chen Shiyuan of the Qing Dynasty), which says, 'By day, produce smoke and by night build a fire and find out where the locusts are located. Several dozen people bring baskets holding ducks, which will eliminate the locusts from all sides.' The optimal time for releasing the ducks was about 20 days before the locusts developed wings. The Notes also mention that one duck was worth one person and that about 40 ducks could eliminate 40,000 locusts. Raising ducks for locust control saves energy and eliminates the need for chemical pesticides, while also reducing the amount of fodder needed by the ducks, thus providing two benefits at once. During the Qing Dynasty (1616-1912), this technique spread to Donghu in Anhui Province and Wuxi in Jiangsu Province and was put to use with great effect." [134][24]

**Figure 4-1 Illustration of ducks raised to control locusts.**

Source: Illustrated History of Ancient Agricultural Techniques of China.

In China, as one can infer from this account, it was from the Ming Dynasty (1368-1644) that ducks were enlisted in the effort to control locusts (grasshoppers, *Orthoptera*, which cause damage to rice plants). Figure 4-1, an illustration of ducks raised to control locusts, shows a scene identical to that which I witnessed in 1992 in Xing'an County, where ducks were being raised in paddy fields. At that time farmers were carrying ducks in exactly that kind of bamboo basket, and I recall seeing a woman bearing them on the same kind of shoulder pole, taking the ducks to a paddy field, where she released them. It is unclear when this illustration was drawn, but it indicates that this scene has been common in China since ancient times. Several things are clear from this illustration.

(1) There were no fences around the paddy fields.

---

[24] Translated by Chen Yangui.

(2) Ducks were released into the paddy fields at times of locust outbreaks. It was not a method of raising ducks and rice plants together as in IRDF.

(3) The ducks they were using were larger than the *aigamo* ducks used in IRDF.

(4) The note specifying that the optimal time for releasing the ducks was twenty days before the locusts developed wings shows they understood the locust life cycle and were releasing ducks in response to it.

In any case, it is clear that ducks have been used to control insect pests in China since the Ming Dynasty.


## 4-1-(2) Raising ducks to control other insects

The following paper was written by Professor Pu Zhelong, an entomologist at Zhongshan University, Guangzhou, China. I met Professor Pu Zhelong at Zhongshan University in 1992.

He wrote, "Raising ducks to control insects and weeds and plough the soil was originally an important measure against pests in rice cultivation in the Pearl River Delta and the surrounding regions in Guangdong Province. It was created through the productive experience of our country's labourers and has a history spanning 600 to 700 years. Using ducks to control pests is effective against a number of different insects that impact rice production, including leafhoppers, planthoppers, cabbage moth larvae (cutworms) and locusts as well as three-brooded rice borers, rice leaf rollers and other harmful insects.

"In order to observe the actual effects of raising ducks for pest control, we conducted an experiment from late 1974 to early 1975 in which ducks were released to control pests. In 1974 we released 30 ducks into an experimental paddy field of 0.83 *mu* (553 m$^2$, 1 *mu* = 666.6 m$^2$) with a high density of locusts, leafhoppers and stinkbugs. We monitored changes in the density of insects prior to and after their release while keeping track of the numbers and kinds of insects in the ducks' stomachs using random sampling. The results are shown in Table 4-1.

"The data in Table 4-1 show that on average, in one hour in the paddy field a duck weighing 0.4 kg would eat 107 insects of 14 varieties. In a further experiment in late 1975, a 0.45 kg duck was found to eat an average of 189 insects an hour, resulting in a decrease in insect pests by 46.7% after one hour; however, 46% of the beneficial insects were also eaten. Thus the ratio of harmful to beneficial insects stayed the same because the ducks were eating roughly equal ratios of each. While they are excellent at controlling insects it has become clear that ducks show great aptitude for removing beneficial insects. This goes against the principle of reducing pests while protecting their natural enemies, but ducks released into a paddy field will control insect pests.

"When ducks are released to control pests, not only do they reduce harmful insects, but they also eat some of the weeds and stir up the soil, thus performing as tillers and weeders as well. In a paddy field with ducks, one intertilling suffices, whereas in fields without ducks it must be done twice. The officials and farmers of Dasha Township value the use of ducks to control pests because raising ducks increases their income and they also benefit from pest and weed control." [134][25]

**Table 4-1. Numbers and types of insect and other pests eaten by ducks released into a rice field.**   (Unit: number of insects)

| Types of insects eaten | Number of insects eaten per duck 30 minutes after release | Number of insects eaten per duck one hour after release | Number of insects eaten per two ducks two hours after release |
|---|---|---|---|
| Rice grasshopper | 19 | 25 | 69 |
| Chinese rice grasshopper | 2 | 4 | 7 |
| Other rice grasshopper | | | 6 |
| Grasshoppers | | | 3 |
| Mole crickets | | | 1 |
| Green rice leafhopper | 1 | | 12 |
| White-backed rice plant hopper | | 3 | 3 |
| Young leafhoppers | | | 16 |
| Adult plant hoppers | 1 | 2 | 3 |
| Young plant hoppers | | | 18 |
| Young leafhoppers and plant hoppers | | | 36 |
| *Cletus trigonus* | 2 | 4 | 12 |
| *Scotinophara lurida* | 3 | 2 | 4 |
| Stinkbug | 1 | | 3 |
| Stibaropus formosanus | 3 | | 5 |
| *Parnara guttata* adults | 1 | | |
| *Parnara guttata* larvae | 1 | 2 | 1 |
| Evening brown (*Mycalesis gotama*) larvae | | | 1 |
| Borers | | 1 | |
| Whirligig beetles | | 1 | |
| Small water beetles | | 7 | 14 |
| Midges | 1 | 7 | |
| River shell (viparus) | | 23 | 80 |
| Kawanina (*Semisulcospina libertina*) | | | 52 |
| Other | | 2 | 4 |
| Spiders | 6 | 16 | 50 |
| Carabids (ground beetles) | | 1 | 2 |
| Ladybug larvae | 1 | | |
| Flies, heads of leafhoppers | | 6 | 24 |
| Small shrimp | | | 1 |
| **TOTAL** | **42** | **107** | **427** |

Source: Professor Pu Zhelong, Overview of Pest Control by Raising Ducks, Dasha Gongshe, Shiquan County, Guangdong Province, 1974

From the above paper, two important points are clear:

(1) The technique of releasing ducks into paddy fields to control pests, remove weeds and till

---

[25] Translated by Chen Yangui.

the soil was invented 600 to 700 years ago by farmers in the Pearl River Delta.

(2) Professor Pu Zhelong was already studying the types and numbers of insect pests eaten per duck over a measured area of paddy fields in 1974.

## 4-1-(3) Domesticated ducks—a natural production system

I received the following paper from Professor Bao Shizeng, an animal husbandry specialist at the South China Agricultural University, whom I visited in 1992. Professor Bao Shizeng was very happy to meet me, saying, "Many Japanese come to our university but you are the first one to inquire about raising ducks in paddy fields."

"China has 320 million domesticated ducks, accounting for 13.3% of its total 2.4 billion domesticated waterfowl. Most are concentrated in the wetlands of the Changjiang (Yangtze) and Pearl River watersheds, where they are being raised by traditional means, released into the broad expanses of paddy fields, ponds, lakes, rivers and reservoirs. Fallen rice ears, aquatic animals and plants, and agricultural pests in the paddy fields comprise their fodder, which is supplemented in response to fluctuations in natural fodder in each season and region to fill their needs for growth and development.

(Passages omitted)

"Renowned breeds in production include the *Zhongshan Ma-ya* duck of Guangdong, the *Peng-ya* duck of Sichuan, the *Gaoyou Ma-ya* duck Jiangsu, the *Shao Ma-ya* duck of Zhejiang, the *Chaohu Ma-ya* duck of Anhui and the *Quanding-ya* duck of Fujian. If we look at the example of Guangdong, where they produce two rice crops a year, the ducks are released while the rice plants are growing in order to till the soil and remove weeds, so they are called 'intertillage ducks'…"[138]

From this we learn that in China, ducks were traditionally raised in the Changjiang and Pearl River watersheds and released into the spacious paddy fields, ponds, lakes and rivers. We also learn they were called "intertillage ducks" because of the role they played in tilling and weeding among the rice plants.

## 4-1-(4) Observations and surveys of the feeding behaviour of free-range ducks

I received the following paper from Professor Zhang Kai at Guangxi Normal University. Professor Zhang Kai conducts research on domesticated ducks.

"Domestic duck breeding has a long history in our country. As far back as the 5th century A.D., during the Southern and Northern Dynasties, the breeding of domesticated ducks was recorded in *Qiminyaoshu* (Complete Techniques Required by the People).

"In *Bencao Gangmu* (Compendium of Materia Medica) by Li Shizhen of the Ming Dynasty, domestic duck breeds, the roles of the drakes and females and artificial insemination methods were described in detail. As I will explain later, the duck breeding industry in our country was already widespread by the time of the Ming Dynasty, and was operated as a kind of secondary production. Since the Ming Dynasty, experience has gradually accumulated and the preferred method has become that of letting the ducks graze and supplementing this with fodder. In other words, flocks of ducks are allowed to graze in the paddy fields, where they eat the insects and wild plants they find there in place of fodder, reducing expenses greatly.

"Since the 1960s, however, double cropping has spread widely and mechanized duck farms have flourished, while the amount of agricultural chemicals used in the paddy fields and the number of times they are sprayed have increased, producing heavier pollution of their food and water, so it has become impossible to continue to release domesticated ducks to graze."[139]

The above provides an example of traditional Chinese duck paddy field grazing. From this we learn four things.

(1) Duck paddy field grazing was the generally employed method of raising domesticated ducks in China.

Ducks were released to range freely in ponds, rivers or paddy fields by day, where they ate naturally-occurring feed, then taken home in the evening and kept in duck sheds. Duck paddy field grazing could be observed anywhere throughout China until the 1960s, as it was the general way of raising ducks. The main objective was not so much to provide a positive effect on the rice, but rather to fatten the ducks.

According to Professor Hu Bai of Ehime University, in parts of Sichuan Province there were fewer paddy fields without domesticated ducks swimming around than there were with them.

(2) The Chinese knew about the effects of ducks

By about 600 to 700 years ago, the Chinese already knew to some extent that ducks performed intertillage, weeding, pest and weed control, and softening and loosening of the soil.

(3) Duck paddy field grazing has declined since the 1960s

This traditional Chinese technology of duck paddy field grazing, however, has declined sharply since the 1960s, when pesticides and chemical fertilizers began to be widely used. Since then the main trend has been to raise ducks in sheds.

The above-mentioned Professor Pu Zhelong of Zhongshan University says, "The Dasha Commune in Siquan County, Guangdong Province, used to raise 200,000 ducks a year. However, the effects of strongly toxic pesticides have reduced their flock by tens of thousands each year. For that reason, farmers have gradually become unable to raise ducks in the paddy fields."[134]

Indeed, a professor I visited in 1992 at Hunan Agricultural University in Changsha, Hunan Province, looked at my slides and expressed concern saying, "In China we use too much pesticide, so wouldn't that have a bad effect on the ducks if we let them go in the paddy fields?"

(4) Artificial insemination of ducks has been practiced since the Ming Dynasty to produce large numbers of ducklings.

## 4-2 Traditional Korean Duck Paddy Field Grazing

Since 1992, I have been asking experts at universities, laboratories and farming families throughout South Korea about their country's traditional duck paddy field grazing. Invariably they tell me something like, "We don't know. We've never heard of it." I still don't know anything about their country's traditional duck paddy field grazing.

## 4-3 Traditional Vietnamese Duck Paddy Field Grazing

Since 1994, when I was first sent to Vietnam by the Japan International Volunteer Centre (JVC), I have visited that country a number of times and have had opportunities to witness traditional duck paddy field grazing in the southern, middle and northern parts of Vietnam.

### 4-3-(1) Outline of duck paddy field grazing in Vietnam

From the results of a questionnaire survey at Hanoi Agricultural University, we found, "About 40 million domesticated ducks are being raised in Vietnam, about one third in the north and two thirds in the south. Traditional paddy field duck breeding has a long history in this country. It is not clear when it started, but it was in ancient times. In 1965, Luong Dinh Cua, who has been called 'the father of modern Vietnamese agriculture,' was said to have taught the Cubans traditional duck paddy field grazing.

"So why did Vietnam's traditional duck paddy field grazing go into decline? A new Cooperative Society system was established in about 1960, which prohibited the pasturing of animals in paddy fields. Ducks were private property but paddy fields were publicly owned, so it was not possible to release them to feed in paddy fields.

"Vietnam has produced three breeds of ducks, the *Co*, *Ky Lua* and *Bau*, and they also breed three foreign types: Pekin, Khaki Campbell and Cherry Valley. The farming method involves releasing them by day and taking them back home in the evening.

"In the north, 60% are raised for meat and 40% for eggs."

The Vietnamese consider ducks' eggs and meat valuable sources of protein, and even during the Vietnam War, farmers let their ducks roam freely. Despite the prohibition on releasing ducks into paddy fields under the Cooperative Society system, they were still released onto waterways and ponds. Later on, the Cooperative Society system was abolished and ducks were once more released into paddy fields. It is clear that in Vietnam the traditional method of duck raising has been passed down and is still continuing.

**4-3-(2) The duck paddy field grazing of Son Thuy Co. (a Cooperative Society) in A Luoi District, Thua Thien-Hue Province**

In 1994 I went to A Luoi District in the mountains of Thua Thien-Hue Province in the central part of Vietnam. Below are the results of a questionnaire survey I conducted at that time.

In this area, farmers release 10- to 15-day-old ducklings into paddy fields one to one-and-a-half months after the rice has been planted. The reason they wait to release the ducklings until a month or more after planting is so that the rice has time to develop strong roots. During that month the rice farmers of this region pull weeds by hand and spray pesticides. The duck farmers do not have their own paddy fields, but release their ducks into other farmers' paddy fields, and when the owners of these fields are going to spray pesticides on fields where the ducks are foraging, they warn the duck farmers and have them remove the ducks from the paddy fields.

In other words, the objective of raising ducks in the paddy fields in A Luoi District is for the ducks to get exercise and find food, and benefits only the duck farmers. It is not based on any positive effects the ducks might have on the growth of the rice plants.

**4-3-(3) Questionnaire survey on traditional duck paddy field grazing**

With the cooperation of JVC Hanoi, I received 24 responses to my questionnaire survey on traditional duck paddy field grazing and IRDF from integrated rice and duck farmers in Haiphong City in the northern part of Vietnam. Their responses regarding traditional duck paddy field grazing can be summarized as follows.

(1) They have been allowing their ducks to forage in paddy fields all along.

(2) Under the traditional method, the ducks ate unhulled rice.

(3) They kept one or two ducks for eggs and these ducks were also released into paddy fields.

(4) Under the traditional method, the ducks were released into paddy fields at random with no prior planning.

(5) They released ducks into the paddy fields in the rainy season,

(6) They kept the ducks in the paddy fields even when harvest time approached.

(7) Under the traditional method, ducks provided a source of income.

(8) Previously, they had also raised ducks in paddy fields, but the period was from one month before harvest to one month after harvest.

(9) Under the traditional method, the ducks were released to forage from two to three months after planting.

(10) Previously, they raised ducks from one month prior to harvest.

From these responses, we understand the following:

Within traditional Vietnamese duck paddy field grazing, one cannot find any particular method that is agreed upon regarding the timing of the ducks' release or their number. What they have in common is the lack of enclosure around paddy fields where the ducks are released. The objective is to raise livestock, i.e., fatten ducks, by letting them eat naturally-occurring weeds, rice plant pests, and so on, in the paddy fields.

## 4-4　Traditional Cambodian Duck Paddy Field Grazing

I met a man in Kampong Cham Province, Cambodia, who was living in a tent pitched on the shore of a lake with lots of fish, where he was raising a flock of 600 domesticated ducks. He would lead his ducks sometimes to paddy fields and sometimes to the lake. In response to my questionnaire survey, he said, "I let the ducks go into the paddy fields only after they begin laying eggs. Paddy fields have lots of feed for them. Ducks smaller than that tend to group together and trample the rice plants, so I can't let them go into the paddy fields. I take the ducks to the paddy fields a month and a half after planting. I don't let them go into the paddy fields when the ears emerge. Right now, I take them to the paddy fields in the morning and the lake in the afternoon."

In surprisingly many cases such as this in Asian duck paddy field grazing, the tiny ducklings are raised at home until they become quite large and then they are released into the paddy fields. The reason for this is the different amounts of feed the ducks need at different stages. Small ducklings do not need a lot of feed, so it is not a burden to keep them at home, but when they get larger, they eat a lot of feed, so they are released into the paddy fields to find naturally-occurring fodder in order to reduce feed costs. Another reason is that it is believed that ducklings group together and trample down the rice plants.

## 4-5　Traditional Indonesian Duck Paddy Field Grazing

Indonesia has four systems for managing duck farming: (1) Extensive farming, (2) Semi-intensive farming, (3) Intensive farming and (4) Industrial farming.
(1) Extensive farming

This is the traditional transhumance system practiced since old times, with no set pastures, but regular transference of livestock according to the seasons.
(2) Semi-intensive farming

This is one typical stock management system widely practiced by Indonesian stockbreeders. It is a cross between the extensive and intensive systems, having been developed somewhat from the extensive system. As Figure 4-2 shows, it consists of a simple duck shed with a simple yard in which the ducks can move around.

**Figure 4-2. Simple shed and yard for semi-intensive farming.**

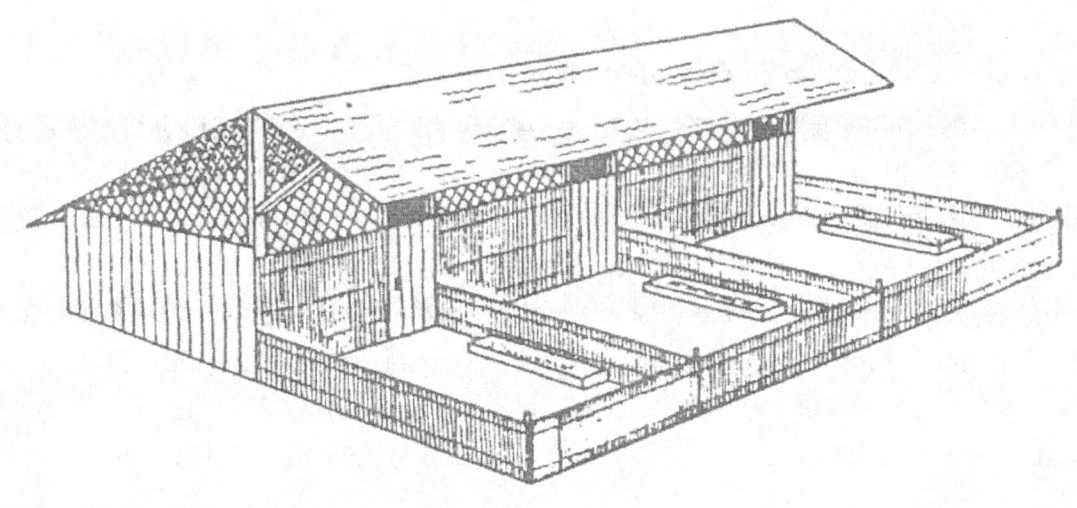

(Source: S.S. Windhyarti, *Beterank Itik Tanpa Air*)

(3) Intensive farming

This type has established feeding and watering facilities that allow all of the ducks to be raised indoors.

**Figure 4-3. Duck-breeding shed for intensive farming.**

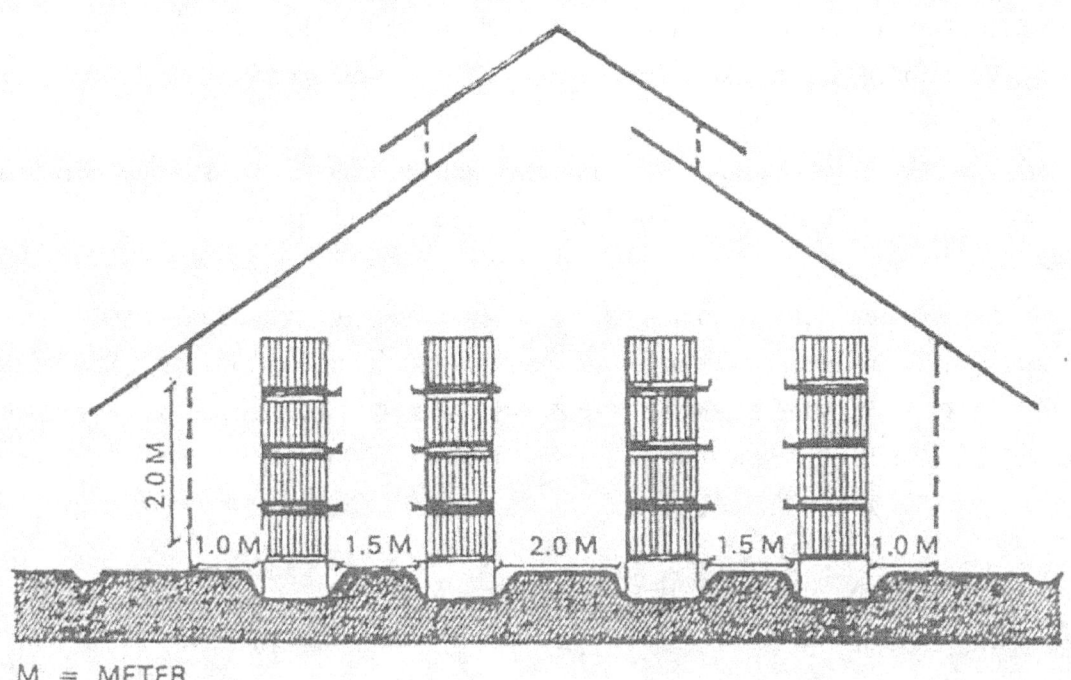

M = METER

(Source: M. Rasyaf, *Beternak Itik Komersial*)

58

(4) Industrial farming

This is large-scale corporate management of duck-breeding.

Of the four types of duck farming systems, the traditional extensive type involved releasing the ducks to feed in paddy fields and was the earliest and most primitive system. It was from this starting point that the other three progressively intensive systems were developed.

In 1993, I collaborated with Professor Masaharu Manda of Kagoshima University and Professor Noboru Fujiwara of Kyushu University to perform local surveys on the Indonesian islands of Java, Bali and Kalimantan (Borneo). At that time, Indonesia ranked third worldwide among duck-producing nations, with 25 million ducks.

We questioned people at the Indonesian Ministry of Agriculture's Department of Livestock Development, Bogor Agricultural University, Diponegoro University, the East Java Livestock Bureau and South Kalimantan Livestock Bureau regarding traditional duck paddy field grazing.

Amazingly, their responses were all the same: "Indonesia's traditional paddy field duck grazing was all post-harvest. We've never heard of anyone releasing ducks into the paddy fields post-planting, when the rice plants were growing."

What we learned from our survey was that for the last half century, traditional Indonesian paddy field duck grazing has been a post-harvest type, with the ducks released into the paddy fields during the day and kept in sheds at night. Among the duck-breeding management systems described above, it is the most primitive type. The modernization of agriculture there in recent years, however, has led to the overuse of pesticides and herbicides, causing duck fatalities and pollution of the unhulled rice they eat on the one hand, and reduced numbers of fish, frogs, shrimp, and so on, on the other. As a result, it has become difficult to pasture ducks in paddy fields post-harvest, and the government recommends that farmers keep their ducks in sheds, using one or another of the more intensive methods that keep the ducks completely separate from the paddy fields. Thus development has proceeded toward more intensive types of duck farming. Under these systems, farmers have to buy fodder. The duck farmers we saw were buying assorted feed from America's Cargill, Inc.

## 4-6  Summary

Indonesian duck farming has developed in connection with traditional rice farming. Until the middle of the 20<sup>th</sup> century, it is said that a form of duck breeding called "*sontoloyo*" was practiced in Java. Under *sontoloyo*, ducks were released into a broad area of rice fields after the rice plants had been cut and were herded from one to the next with the family coming along for the journey. Under modernized livestock breeding systems, the livestock are generally kept in sheds and provided fodder by humans. Under the *sontoloyo* method, both humans and their livestock ranged about in search of forage. This could be considered an energy-saving type of livestock breeding.

When we hear the term "nomadic" we tend to think of Mongolian sheep herders. *Sontoloyo* could be considered as a kind of nomadism of Asia's rice growing regions.

Prior to WWII, I hear there were nomadic duck herders on China's Hainan Island. They wandered with their ducks along the banks of rivers. By the time they reached the mouth of the river at Haikou City, the ducks were fat and the herders would sell them and go back home.

Until recently, in Thua Thien-Hue Province in central Vietnam, a form of duck transhumance called "*nui vit chay tang*" was also practiced.

The feeding method used in duck transhumance is to release the ducks into paddy fields where the rice plants have been harvested. Paddy field duck breeding, including post-harvest pasturing (bird tillage) was the normal method of duck farming common across Asia. Not only were ducks released, but also goats, water buffalo, pigs, chickens and other livestock were pastured in cultivated fields, grasslands, rivers and ponds on a daily basis from ancient times. Even now, if you go to the mountains of Vietnam, the vegetable fields and seedling beds are surrounded by bamboo fences. This is done to protect the plants from being eaten by water buffalo, pigs, chickens and ducks that are allowed to wander.

It is becoming impossible, however, to continue this traditional kind of duck pasturing because of the modernization of agriculture, which uses large amounts of pesticides, herbicides and chemical fertilizers. This is happening throughout Asia, not only in China, Vietnam and Indonesia, as we have mentioned here.

Even the 2004 issue of *Dao-ya Gongsheng* (Rice and Duck Symbiosis), published by Anhui Province in China, says, "Duck paddy field grazing has a long history in our country and is the fruit of traditional Chinese agriculture. Through long years of practical experience since ancient times, our country's farmers have found that raising ducks in paddy fields protects them against disease-carrying insects and also has other functions such as weed control, soil loosening and fertility enhancement" [93]. I think that is certainly true.

In the light of my own experience, however, this discovery in the context of Asia's rich and serene waterfowl culture differs in its nature from what are considered "discoveries" in the modern era. What I mean is that if you have ducks and paddy fields, the ducks will naturally enter the paddy fields and eat the weeds and insects they find. The people in Asian countries naturally made use of this tendency in livestock breeding and rice production. That is to say, it was not so much that somebody in some country had the idea of releasing ducks into paddy fields to feed and then this idea was transmitted across Asia as a great discovery, but rather it would be more natural to consider it as having arisen spontaneously in each country and region where ducks and paddy fields coexisted.

In other words, traditional paddy field pasturing was carried out by allowing ducks to roam freely in paddy fields with no enclosures. The objective was not so much to achieve a good effect on rice plants as it was to fatten the ducks. The effects of the ducks on the rice plants, however, such as pest control, weeding and tilling, were recognized from the start. In recent years, though, the modernization of agriculture has brought about the use of pesticides, herbicides and chemical fertilizers, making it difficult to pasture ducks in paddy fields.

This traditional agricultural method of duck paddy field grazing is economical and rational because the ducks eat naturally-occurring fodder. This is because the ducks can eat freely in an unenclosed space. Since IRDF involves a limited space, it limits the amount of natural fodder the ducks can obtain.

The ducks that escape from our family's enclosed duck paddy field eat up the golden snails in our neighbours' paddy fields. If it weren't for the enclosure, the ducks would be able to eat all the pests and weeds they wanted.

# Chapter 5
## The Various Forms of Integrated Rice and Duck Farming (IRDF) in Asia

In 1992 I visited China and Taiwan and reported on the theory and practice of IRDF to rice farmers, duck farmers, agricultural leaders and researchers. Since then I have been continuing the 'aigamo farmer exchanges' through opportunities to visit rural areas in many countries including Indonesia, Vietnam, South Korea, China, Taiwan, Cambodia, and Malaysia.

At present, IRDF is developing and diffusing through a process of adaptation to the natural and socioeconomic conditions in each local region. The intention of this chapter is to summarize, mainly from the viewpoint of techniques, the regional characteristics of these diverse and developing integrated rice and (domesticated) duck farming methods, and the points they have in common.

### 5-1 IRDF in China

The Fourth Asian Aigamo Symposium was held in Zhenjiang City, Jiangsu Province, China on 21 July 2004. In the sponsor's greeting at the beginning of the symposium, Mr. Feng Huaisong, a departmental director in the Chinese Ministry of Agriculture, reported that in that year rice and duck farming had expanded to 20,000 ha throughout the country. 20,000 ha was roughly the same as the area of wet rice cultivation in the whole of Kyushu island for that year. Since integrated duck and rice farming was first introduced into China from Japan in 1999, this was a surprising expansion in a mere five years. Table 5-1 shows the areas to which duck and rice farming had diffused in China in 2006.

### Table 5-1. Rice and Duck Farming Areas in China, 2006

| Province | Area (ha) | |
|---|---|---|
| Jiangsu | 960 | Notes: Data provided by Mr. Shen Shaokun of the Science and Technology Bureau of Zhenjiang City. However, this does not represent accurate statistical data. Data for Anhui Province provided by Mr. Xiong Guoyuan of the Livestock and Grassland Veterinary Research Institute of the Anhui Province Academy of Agricultural Science. In addition, IRDF has also spread to Hubei, Guangdong, Liaoning and other provinces, but implemented areas have not been surveyed. |
| Zhejiang | 33,300 | |
| Anhui | 30,000 | |
| Hunan | 54,000 | |
| Sichuan | 16,000 | |
| Jilin | 300 | |
| Heilongjiang | 100 | |
| Henan | 66 | |
| Xinjiang | 100 | |
| TOTAL | 134,826 | |

Many names are used for IRDF in China. In Jiangsu Province it is known as *dao-ya gong zuo* (rice and ducks work together), in Anhui and Yunnan Provinces it is called *dao-ya gong sheng* (rice and ducks live together), in Sichuan Province *dao-ya gong qi* (rice and ducks stay together), and in Beijing it is called *dao-ya gong yu* (rice and ducks swim together). For convenience, and in order to distinguish it from the traditional technique of *daotian yangya* (duck paddy field grazing), I will generally use the term *dao-ya gong zuo* (rice and ducks work together). I will also explain the Sichuan technique of *dao-ya gong qi* (rice and ducks stay together) in more detail later in the chapter.

## 5-2 Background to the Development of Rice and Duck Farming in China

As mentioned above, I visited China to introduce the ideas of IRDF for the first time in 1992. For about ten years after that, however, I received absolutely no reports of IRDF spreading in that country. Nevertheless, in 1999 and 2000 I visited Jiangsu, Anhui and Hunan Provinces for *aigamo* exchanges. The direct catalyst for this was that around 1999, as a part of the 'Campaign to Send Japanese Books on Japanese Agriculture to China' being implemented by the Japanese publisher the Rural Culture Association, two of my books, *Aigamo Banzai* and *The Infinite Spread of Integrated Duck and Rice Culture* were sent to the Science and Technology Association of Zhenjiang City, Jiangsu Province, where they caught the eye of Mr. Shen Shaokun and Mr. Wang Zhiqiang.

As can be seen from the case studies in Jiangsu, Anhui and Heilongjiang Provinces in Table 5-2, rice and duck farming as it is currently practiced in China uses nets to enclose the paddy fields and releases 20 to 30 domesticated ducks (one to two weeks old) into each 10 ares one to two weeks after seedling transplantation. As far as the basic techniques are concerned, they are exactly the same as those of IRDF carried out in Japan. However, in contrast to Japan, the process is not always pesticide-free and there are cases where small amounts of pesticides and chemical fertilizers are used as needed. In addition, prevention of loss from external predators is carried out simply by enclosing large areas of paddy fields with netting.

In the summer of 2001, I had an opportunity to visit fields where rice and duck farming was being practiced while at a rice and duck conference in Anhui Province. Ducks of a large domesticated duck variety known as *suhu maya* were swimming about in a paddy field where the ears had just begun to emerge on the rice plants. The rice was a strong, high-yield variety and a sign reading "Green Rice and Duck Farming Model Area" had been set up at the roadside, where a large number of visitors had gathered.

Although not one of the case studies covered in the survey, Jianhua Village, Longtang Township, Feisu County, Anhui Province is the largest rice and duck collective in the province. The planted area is 200 ha, of which the government has granted subsidies for netting and other materials for 100 ha. Farmers began to carry out rice and duck farming independently on the other 100 ha. On the former, 12 rice farming families were producing rice on 100 ha. Making use of those paddy fields, three duck farming households had enclosed the fields in nets and were raising 30,000 ducks through rice and duck farming. The ducks ate the natural food available in the paddy fields and it was reported that savings of

10% to 30% were made on feed costs. This was what made it worthwhile for the duck farmers.

**Table 5-2. Implementation Details of Rice and Duck Farming in Three Provinces of China**

| | Yanling Town, Danyang City, Jiangsu Province | Anhui Province | Mr. Hong Xiangshao, Heilongjiang Province |
|---|---|---|---|
| Area (ha) | 430 | 30,000 | 10 |
| Employed labour (cap.) | 25 | 50,000 | 3 |
| Enclosure material | Nylon net | Netting[1] | Netting[1] |
| Number of ducks per 10 ares | 20 | 30 | 25 |
| Age of ducklings at time of release (weeks) | 1.5 | 1 | 2 |
| Cost per duckling (yuan) | 12 | 6.3 | 7 |
| Chemical fertilizer input (kg/ha) *Aigamo* fields Conventional fields | None 100 | 10 40 | None Unknown |
| Pesticide input (kg/ha) *Aigamo* fields Conventional fields | None 2.25 | Twice[2] Six times | None 0.2 |
| Herbicide input (kg/ha) *Aigamo* fields Conventional fields | None 0.045 | None Twice[2] | None |
| *Aigamo* effects [Weed suppression (a), insect pest suppression (b), stimulation (c) only] | (a) Sufficient (b) Insufficient (c) Extremely good | (a) Insufficient (b) Insufficient (c) Extremely good | (a) Sufficient (b) Sufficient (c) Slight effect |
| Rice yield (kg/10 ares) *Aigamo* fields Conventional fields | 610 630 | 536 512 | 400 500 |
| Sales price of *genmai* (yuan/kg) *Aigamo* fields Conventional fields | 3.4 2.8 | 1.2 0.8 | 10-16 2.82 |
| *Aigamo*/Conventional ratios | | | |
| Yield ratio[3] | 0.96 | 1.04 | 0.8 |
| Price ratio[4] | 1.21 | 1.5 | 3.54-5.67 |
| Sales value ratio[5] | 0.11 | 0.35 | 0.22-0.04 |

Source: Prepared by the author from the 2006 questionnaire survey.
Notes: 1. Material unknown, 2. Amount unknown, *genmai* = brown rice
3. Yield ratio = yield (kg) / 10 ares of *aigamo* field ÷ yield (kg) / 10 ares of conventional field,
4. Price ratio = Selling price of rice produced in *aigamo* field ÷ Selling price of rice produced in conventional field,
5. Sales value ratio = Income from sale of ducks per 10 ares ÷ Income from sale of rice per 10 ares.

**Figure 5-1. Cultivation calendar for rice and duck farming in Yanling Town, Danyang City, Jiangsu Province**

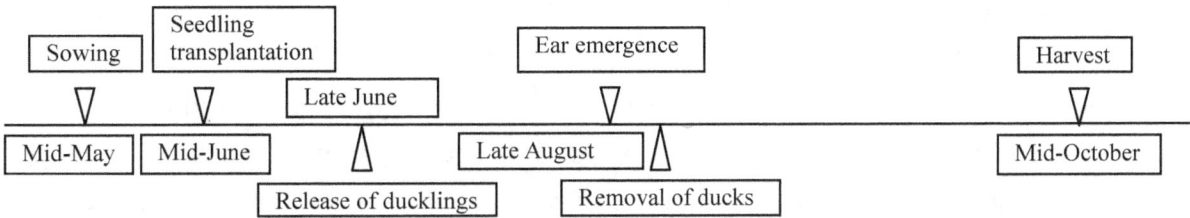

Source: Prepared by the author from the 2006 questionnaire survey.

**Figure 5-2. Cultivation calendar for rice and duck farming by Mr. Hong Xiangshao, Heilongjiang Province**

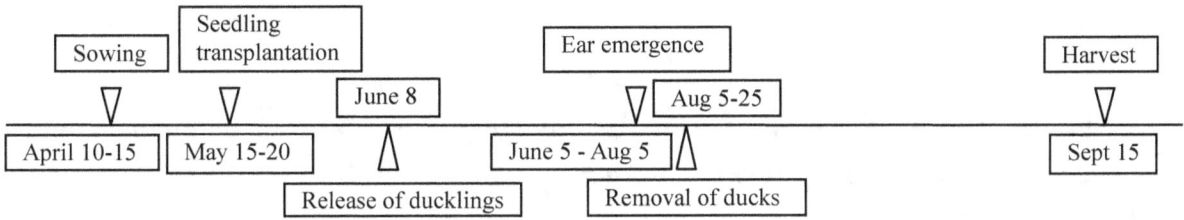

Source: Prepared by the author from the 2006 questionnaire survey.

Since the raising and managing of the ducks was completely handled by the duck farmers, life was also made easier for the rice farmers. According to Mr. Xiong Guodao of the livestock research institute, who was supervising the rice and duck farming in the village, "Using this method, yields have increased by 30 kg per *mu (1 mu = 666.7 m², 6.667 ares)*. Economically speaking, 30 yuan profit (1 yuan is about 16 US cents) has been gained from the increase in yield and 70 yuan from the reduction in the use of chemical fertilizers and pesticides. Insect pests have been reduced by 70% and rice diseases have declined 88%."

When Japanese "IRDF" is introduced into China, the operational methods and scale become completely different, as in this case. This is the power of the traditions of China, where there is an unbroken line of 3,000 years of history of waterfowl culture and where 661 million ducks are kept (2002). Despite 30,000 ducks being released on 100 ha of paddy field with just a simple net for enclosure there are no losses from external predators. Viewed in the light of our experience in Japan, this is quite unbelievable. In Japan, crows, dogs, foxes and weasels would be queuing up to attack the ducks. There is a necessity for further study on just exactly how the three duck farming households raise and manage 30,000 ducks.

"In Vietnam, dogs kept near people's houses almost never attack ducks. If a dog eats a duck, people will eat the dog. This is a kind of dog breeding history that we have in Vietnam." This was something I heard in Haiphong, Vietnam, in 1994. The situation is probably quite similar in China.

**5-3 A Summary of Techniques Used in Rice and Duck Farming in Sichuan Province, China**

In Sichuan Province, enclosing paddy fields with bamboo fences and releasing ducks into the paddy fields, known as *dao-ya gongqi*, began around 1988 to 1990. I heard a report about this at the 4th Asian *Aigamo* Symposium, held in Zhenjiang City, Jiangsu Province in 2004. If this is true, it suggests that "IRDF" had also begun independently in China. 1988 is the year in which I first met *aigamo* ducks. I felt a historical flow of time that seemed to go beyond a mere coincidental timing of events.

Sometime later, the Science and Technology Association of Zhenjiang City sent me a book entitled *Daotian zonghe fazhan* (*The Comprehensive Development of Paddy Fields*) in which there was some information about the *dao-ya gongxi* of Sichuan Province. I found the contents very interesting and I would like to give a brief introduction of the method here, based on this book.

**5-4 A Summary of Techniques Used in Rice and Duck Farming in Sichuan Province from *The Comprehensive Development of Paddy Fields***
　**5-4-(1) Types of rice and duck farming**

(1) Duck raising by dispersed farmers
　One farming household raises ten or fewer ducks in a paddy field. Ducks are taken to the paddy field in the morning and returned to the shed near the farmhouse in the evening.
(2) Large-scale duck raising
　The number of ducks is not fixed, being 30 to 200 ducks per household. Owing to the large numbers of ducks, there are people who specialize in looking after the ducks, and who take the ducks to the fields in the morning and bring them back to the sheds in the evening. The ecological and economic effect is clearly greater than for the dispersed farmers.
(3) *Dao-ya gongqi* – rice and ducks stay together, or duck raising in the paddy fields
　Ducks are released and raised at a density of about 20 to 25 ducks per *mu*. The ducks do not return to the house in the evening but are left as they are in the paddy field.
(4) Rice-duck-fish 3D production
(5) Duck raising with paddy field boards
　In general, ducklings are released into the paddy fields after the rice harvest. A scale of about 300 to 500 ducklings is usual, but in some cases may exceed 800. The "boards" are for the person who lives out in the fields, looks after the ducks, and moves around with them. This is rather like a tent in a camping ground.

Rice and duck farming in Sichuan Province can be broken down roughly into the above five types. Of these, type (3) *Dao-ya gongqi* – duck raising in the paddy fields, is the type that has diffused to the greatest degree. Below I will clarify the main technical points and merits of rice and duck farming in Sichuan Province on the basis of type (3).

## 5-4-(2) Main technical points

The techniques of *dao-ya gongqi* were developed by researchers such as Mr. Gu Yichen at the Zhanzhou Rice Research Institute of the Agricultural Science College of Sichuan Province. Ducks are released into the paddy fields at a density of 20 to 25 ducks per *mu*. Each duck weighs about 1.5 kg by the time it is sold, and thus 30 to 40 kg of duck are produced. Although the data is incomplete, in the southeastern region of Sichuan Province alone the planted area has expanded to about 150,000 to 200,000 *mu* (10,000 to 13,340 ha), on which three to four million ducks are raised.

Since in this technique the ducks are raised in the field and not taken home in the evening, the greatest worry for the farmer is duck thieves, and there have been difficulties in extending this technique to farmers who have paddy fields dispersed here and there over a large area. Because of this, it has been found effective to carry out *dao-ya gongqi* by forming production bases involving all the farmers in one area through extension and promotion activities carried out by local administrative organizations. Areas of 20,000 *mu* (1334 ha) of *dao-ya gongqi* fields were formed in a number of townships in Huaqiao District and Guange District, Guangan County, Sichuan Province in 1990.

*Dao-ya gongqi* involves returning ducks to nature, allowing them to live freely in the paddy fields, for the purposes of making the greatest use possible of the natural food in the paddy field, taking advantage of the effects of integrating rice plants and ducks, and increasing profits by reducing production costs. The main technical features of *dao-ya gongqi* are as follows.

(1) Selection of paddy fields. Since these are terraced fields in a hilly region, fields with an area of over one *mu*, with a low ridge in front and a high ridge or wall at the back are ideal. In this case, the merits are that the use of fencing materials is reduced and all the fields of the local farmers can be used in the implementation of *dao-ya gongqi*. In the case of paddy fields on flat land, the fields must be enclosed with nets.

(2) Selection of the rice variety and transplantation density. High-quality seeds of a large rice plant variety are selected and transplanted with a slightly larger than normal distance between seedlings, known as sparse planting. The merit of sparse planting is that since the ducks pass between the rice plants in *dao-ya gongqi*, the ducks are able to be more freely active and the rice seedlings are not trampled down. For example, using the II Fine 6078 rice variety bred at the Chongqing City Crop Institute, 10,000 plants are planted per *mu* and the

yield has reached as high as 550 to 600 kg/*mu*. Since temperature and light differ in different regions, this can be adjusted within the quite large range of 8,000 to 14,000 plants per *mu*. Sichuan Province's Hill Fine 22, II Fine 838, Chongqing's You Fine No.6 and other varieties have achieved yields of 500 to 550 kg/*mu* with planting densities of 13,000 to 15,000 seedlings per *mu* in the southeastern region of Sichuan Province.

(3) Selection of the duck variety. In Sichuan Province in general the duck varieties *gaoyouya, jianchangya, Sichuan ma-ya*, varieties producing both meat and eggs, are selected as ducks which can be raised outdoors. These ducks are of about medium size, have good predatory ability and are very adaptable.

(4) Incubation of chicks and prevention of disease. The timing of hatching has to be linked closely with the transplantation of the rice seedlings. In general, since the ducklings are released into the paddy field seven days after seedling transplantation, when the rice plants have taken strong root, calculating backwards the chicks should be hatching about 15 days before that, and counting backwards again a further 28 days gives the date for starting the incubation of the eggs. In Chongqing City, egg incubation generally begins from mid to late March. After hatching, it is necessary to have the chicks swallow medicine for disease prevention. The newborn chicks are raised at the house for about 20 days, and when they have reached a weight of about 200g are released into the paddy fields. About seven to ten days before release they are injected, again for disease prevention purposes.

(5) Fence-making and constructing a resting place for the ducks. Since the ducks will be outside for a long period, unless their range of activity is fixed within certain limits the ducks will move around at will, making management difficult. The usual way of handling this is to build a fence around the paddy field. If the ridge at the rear of the paddy field is high then only the front ridge needs to be fenced, but if the rear ridge is also low then it will be necessary to enclose the whole paddy field in a fence. Bamboo is usually used for this and the fences are erected to about 45 cm in height and slightly leaning in towards the paddy field. In order to reduce costs, bamboo stakes are fixed into the ridge at two-meter intervals and a net strung between them. A bush with thorns, like a briar bush, is sometimes planted around a paddy field as a fence.

The ducks cannot live in the water all the time and need to come up onto the land to rest from time to time. In some places a duck shed is built next to the paddy field for this, but considering costs and security (from theft) almost all the resting places are built in the paddy field as earth platforms.

(6) Use of azolla. At the same time as growing azolla in the paddy field to fix nitrogen, the azolla is an important source of food for the ducks. Seed azolla is put into the field at the rate of 200 kg/*mu* about seven days after seedling transplantation. Following that, fertilizer containing $Ca(H_2PO_4)_2 \cdot H_2O$ (calcium superphosphate), $CaSO_4$ (calcium sulphate), $H_3PO_4$ (phosphoric acid) is spread in the field each week at the rate of about five kg/*mu*.

(7) Number and timing of release of ducklings. In general, 20 to 25 ducklings are released

per *mu* of paddy field. If 15 or fewer ducklings are released, they do not need to be given extra feed, but above that number supplementary feed is necessary. No more than 30 ducklings are released per *mu* of paddy field.

(8) Taking care of the ducks. After releasing the ducklings into the paddy field the ducklings and the situation in the paddy field should be monitored frequently. The level of water in the paddy field should be properly managed and the fence repaired to prevent ducklings escaping. If 20 or more ducklings are released per *mu* of paddy field, it is necessary to provide supplementary feed every evening. The supplementary feed mix given as an example by the Zhanzhou Rice Research Institute is maize 62%, wheat bran 20%, fried broad beans 6%, fish meal 3%, oil cake 4%, bonemeal 2.8%, silkworm pupae 2%, salt 0.2%. While the ducks are being kept outside, one person must be delegated to take care of the ducks. When the ducks have grown to about 1.5 kg in weight they are all removed from the paddy field and sold or further fattened.

### 5-4-(3) Effects

(1) The ducks grow quickly. The evening supplementary feed is added to the food found in the paddy field during the day. The nutritional balance is good and the ducks therefore grow quickly. According to statistics from Jiangjin County, ducks that have grown along with an early rice variety grow to an average weight of 1.6 kg 81 days after release into the field. Subtracting the body weight of 200 g at the time of release into the paddy field, the body weight increases at an average rate of 17.3 g/day. Ducks that have grown with a late rice variety grow to an average weight of 1.75 kg 62 days after release into the paddy field. Subtracting the body weight of 200 g at the time of release into the paddy field, the body weight increases at an average rate of 25 g/day. The rate of increase of body weight is clearly greater in the latter than in the former. The reason for this is thought to be that temperatures are higher in the autumn and that food such as insects, weeds, fallen rice seeds, fish, shrimp, and mud snails are more plentiful in the paddy field in the later period.

(2) Low cost, high profit. Compared with the method of taking the ducks home to a duck shed for the night this method of keeping the ducks in the paddy field for 24 hours a day requires less than one-third of the supplemental feed. The main costs are expenditures for the chicks and the fences, amounting to about 50 yuan per *mu* in total for the two periods of duck raising, the early rice period and the late rice period. If the number of ducks 'harvested' is 40 and each duck has an average body weight of 1.6 kg, then the total weight will be 64 kg. The unit price is 8 yuan/kg and so the income from ducks will be 512 yuan, minus costs of 50 yuan gives a net profit of 462 yuan per *mu*.

(3) Duck health and hygiene of the house yard are secured. If the ducks were returning to sheds at night, unpleasant smells would arise from droppings on the road, and this would also have an unfavourable influence on the hygiene of the house yard. Keeping the ducks outside in the paddy fields, however, as well as providing them with a comfortable living space and

ensuring their health, also secures a hygienic living environment for the owner and his or her neighbours.

(4) Large room for expansion. The adaptability of *dao-ya gongqi* – duck raising in the field – is great and it is suitable for either single cropping or double cropping of rice each year. [131][26]


## 5-5 Why is *Dao-ya Gongqi* Included in *Daotian Yangya?*

In this book (*The Comprehensive Development of Paddy Fields*), *dao-ya gongqi*, in which ducks are released into paddy fields enclosed with a fence, is included as one type of *daotian yangya*, traditional duck paddy field grazing in which ducks are released into paddy fields that are not enclosed with a fence and are allowed to move around freely. From the drift of the argument thus far this seems rather strange, but if you read the book carefully the reason for this becomes apparent.

The reason given in the book for setting up a fence around paddy fields is that unless you do so the active range of the ducks will not be limited and therefore it will become difficult to manage the ducks.

The book goes on to mention the following three effects of *dao-ya gongqi*.

(1) Fast growth of ducks,

(2) Low cost due to only one-third of the supplementary feed required,

(3) Health of the ducks and hygiene.

All of these effects are from the viewpoint of livestock. There is no mention of the positive enhancement of '*aigamo* effects' on the rice plants by releasing ducks into a limited space. In other words, this is the same as *daotian yangya*, in which livestock are the main focus. That is probably why *dao-ya gong qi* is included in this book as one type of *daotian yangya*.

Rather than ask the author of the book, it may be necessary to ask Mr. Gu Yicheng of the Zhanzhou Rice Research Institute of the Agricultural Science College of Sichuan Province, and the originator of the *dao-ya gongqi* technique, to know whether this is indeed the case. In any event, the fact that rice fields were being enclosed with bamboo fences around 1990 is very interesting. Further exchanges and enquiry are necessary.


## 5-6 IRDF in South Korea

### 5-6-(1) Background

Korean IRDF began in 1992 when the president of the Tokyo Branch of the Busan Ilbo (Busan Daily) news agency, Mr. Choi Soeng Kyu and his businessman brother-in-law, Mr. Kim Tae Nyon began training under the Furunos' guidance, but it was due to the efforts of members of the Chong Nong Hui (Right Agriculture Association), especially the former principal of Poolmoo Agriculture Technical High School, Mr. Hong Sun Myong, and farmers'

---

[26] Translated by Chen Yangui.

leader, Mr. Chu Hyang Ro, that it actually became established throughout South Korea. Among South Korea's numerous organic agricultural organizations, the Chong Nong Hui is said to have been the ground-breaker in the organic farming movement.

It was in mid-summer 1994 that I first met Mr. Hong Sun Myong in Changnyong, Gyeongsangnam Province. Since then, activities of the Chong Nong Hui, with the central participation of Mr. Chu Hyang Ro and Mr. Hong Sun Myong, in promoting IRDF have been notable.

According to the Korea Federation of Sustainable Agriculture Organizations, headquartered in Seoul, about 7,400 South Korean farming households were engaged in IRDF in 2005, involving about 6,300 ha, the area having increased by a factor of five in five years.

IRDF in Hongdong Township, Hongseong County, is based on the form practiced in Japan. There are two differences, however. One is in not using electric fences to protect the ducks from predators as is done in Japan. Rather, at night the ducks are kept in a sturdy steel shed occupying a corner of the paddy field and are released into the field again by day. IRDF in South Korea is organized into collectives, and *aigamo* residential complexes have been built. There are extremely few cases of individual farmers practicing the technique on their own, as is normal in Japan. This is because in South Korea, subsidies are provided to collectives. The steel sheds are all prefabricated and purchased using subsidies. Another difference is in the timing of the release of ducklings into the paddy fields. The farming calendar sets the ducklings' release at the beginning of June and removal at the end of July, but on July 10, 2006, the ducklings were already being removed from the paddy fields. In South Korea, ducks are customarily eaten at midsummer, so they are taken from the fields at that time and handed over to traders. This is why the ducks were being removed from the paddy fields so early.

For reference, in Japan the ducklings are released at the beginning of June and removed from the paddy fields in mid to late August.

Table 5-3 gives details on the IRDF of Hongdong Township, where Poolmoo Agriculture Technical High School is located and Mr. Chu Hyang Ro and Mr. Hong Sun Myong reside. The figures for values per 10 ares and per kilogram are averages. The reasons why the ducks failed to be sufficiently effective at weeding were thought to be that the rice seedlings were small and the release of the ducklings was delayed. The collective plans to introduce planting machines that handle more mature seedlings in 2007.

**Table 5-3. Example of IRDF in Hongdong Township, Hongseong County, Chungcheongnam Province, South Korea.**

| | Hongseong County, Chungcheongnam Province |
|---|---|
| Area cultivated | 900 ha |
| Labour force | 1,020 |
| Enclosure | Net, kept in steel shed at night |
| No. of ducklings/10a | 15 to 20 |
| Duckling size | 10 days |
| Value/duck | 1800 won* |
| Chemical fertilizer/ha | None in duck fields |
| Pesticides/10a | None in duck fields |
| Herbicides/10a | None in duck fields |
| Effects of ducks | Insufficient against weeds such as barnyard millet (*Echinochloe esculenta*), arrowhead (*Eleocharis dulcis*) and water plantain (*Sagittaria trifolia*); sufficient pest control; some stimulation |
| Rice yield/10a | 550 kg from duck fields; 550 kg from conventional fields |
| Rice value/kg | 3500 won from duck fields; 2000 won from conventional fields |
| Yield ratio | 1 |
| Price ratio | 1.75 |
| Sales value ratio | 0.018 |

\* 1 won is about 0.1 US cent
Source: Prepared by the author from the 2006 questionnaire survey.

**Figure 5-3. IRDF calendar (Hongdong Township, Hongseong County, Chungcheongnam Province).**

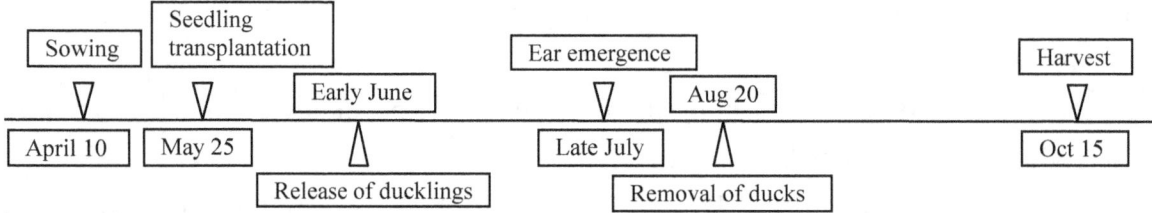

Source: Prepared by the author from the 2006 questionnaire survey.

Figure 5-3 shows a typical example of an IRDF calendar for Hongdong Township, Hongseong County, Chungcheongnam Province.

## 5-7 IRDF in Vietnam

"Vietnamese farmers are poor. They grow only rice and their yields are meagre. Under these conditions, this would be an effective way to break away from rice monocropping. The household incomes of all of the families trying it are rising. Until now ducks have been considered harmful to rice. In today's talk, we found out that they are beneficial." This was the appraisal of one Vietnamese farmer after hearing a lecture on IRDF at the SAP (Sustainable Agriculture Promotion) Centre in Haiphong City.

In 1994 my wife and I, together with Professor Masaharu Manda of Kagoshima University and his wife were dispatched to Vietnam by JVC. Our visit provided the stimulus for the launching of IRDF with domesticated ducks in various parts of the country, including Ho Chi Minh City, Ben Tre Province and Dong Thap Province in the south, Thua Thien-Hue Province in central Vietnam, and Hanoi City, Hai Phong Province, Bac Giang Province and Hoa Binh Province in the north.

Since then, IRDF has spread out from the regions in which JVC is active. If we take the example of IRDF under the natural and social conditions of northern Vietnam, a densely populated region where farmers cultivate about 20 to 30 ares per household, we can see that it develops in characteristic ways. Below I will present examples of farming families in Chien Thang Village, An Lao County, Hai Phong City, and provide information on the details of three business operations and three farming calendars (Figs. 5-4 to 5-6).

**Table 5-4. IRDF business operation in Chien Thang Village, An Lao County, Hai Phong City.**

| Name of farmer | Ngo Quang Bang | Pham Thi Hanh | Pham Van Phong |
|---|---|---|---|
| Area utilized | 2000 m$^2$ | 20,000 m$^2$ | 10,000 m$^2$ |
| Labour force | 2 people | 3 people | 3 people |
| Enclosure | Concrete | Nylon and bamboo | Polyethylene |
| No. of ducklings/10a | 100 | 100 | 100 |
| Duckling size | 12 days | 12 days | 15 days |
| Value/duck | 19,000 dong | 20,000 dong | 22,000 dong |
| Chemical fertilizer/ha | None in duck fields | Duck fields: n/s | None in duck fields |
| | 80 kg in conventional fields | Conventional fields: n/s | 195 kg in conventional fields |
| Pesticides/ha | 0.2 kg in duck fields | Duck fields: n/s | None in duck fields |
| | 0.5 kg in conventional fields | Conventional fields: n/s | 0.2 kg in conventional fields |
| Herbicides/ha | None in duck fields | Duck fields: n/s | None in duck fields |
| | 0.1 kg in conventional fields | Conventional fields: n/s | 0.2 kg in conventional fields |
| Effects of ducks | Sufficient against weeds | Sufficient against weeds | Against weeds: n/s |
| | Sufficient against pests | Sufficient against pests | Insufficient against pests |
| | Stimulation: n/s | Stimulation: n/s | Stimulation: n/s |
| Rice yield/10a | 450 kg from duck fields | 450 kg from duck fields | 400 kg from duck fields |
| | 450 kg from conventional fields | 450 kg from conventional fields | 450 kg from conventional fields |
| Rice value/kg | 3500 dong from duck fields | 6800 dong from duck fields | 5000 dong from duck fields |
| 3600 dong from conventional fields | 6000 dong from conventional fields | 4000 dong from conventional fields | |

n/s: not surveyed or unknown

Source: Prepared by the author from the 2006 questionnaire survey.

**Figure 5-4 IRDF calendar of Mr. Pham Van Phong (winter-spring crop only).**

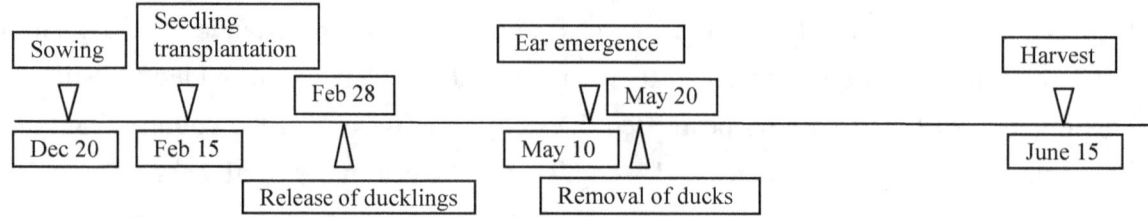

Source: Prepared by the author from the 2006 questionnaire survey.


**Figure 5-5 IRDF calendar of Mr. Pham Van Bar (winter-spring crop only).**

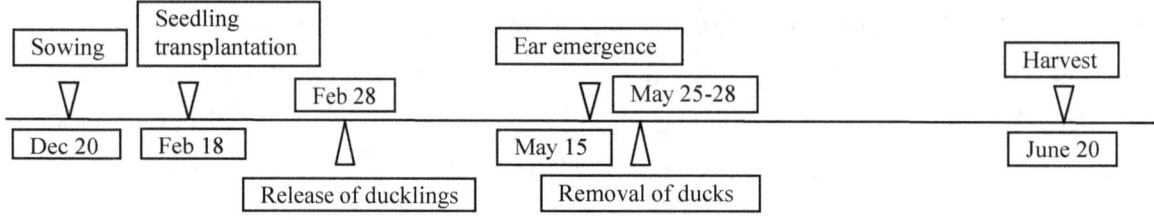

Source: Prepared by the author from the 2006 questionnaire survey.


**Figure 5-6 IRDF calendar of Mr. Nuyen The Phiet (winter-spring crop only).**

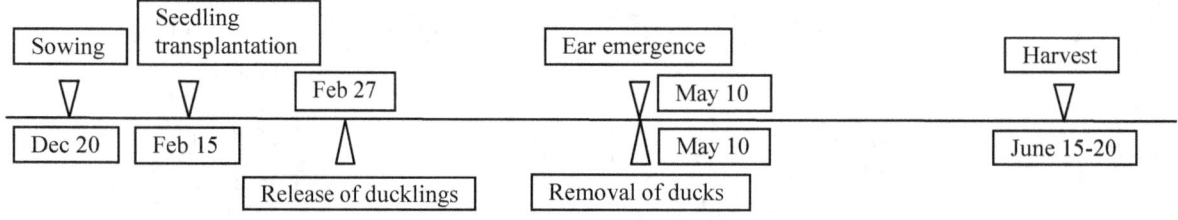

Source: Prepared by the author from the 2006 questionnaire survey.


As can be seen from these three examples of farming calendars, the farmers of Chien Thang Village, An Lao County, Hai Phong City transfer the rice seedlings to the paddy fields on about the 55th day after sowing the seedlings for the winter-spring crop. Ducklings are released into the paddy fields within two weeks of transplanting and then removed once the rice ears emerge. The IRDF practiced here is based on the method introduced from Japan. As is clear from Table 5-4, the difference between the method practiced in Vietnam and the Japanese method is in the number of ducklings released. In Japan, China or South Korea, roughly 15 to 30 ducklings are released per 10 ares. I drafted Table 5-5 in order to find out if this practical detail was limited to Chien Thang Village alone. It can be seen from the table that the average areas cultivated by collectives practicing IRDF was 6,855 m$^2$ in Chien Thang Village, 5,266 m$^2$ in Quoc Tuan Village and 2,784 m$^2$ in Hoa Nghia Village, showing clear differences from place to place.

**Table 5-5. Differences in IRDF in Hai Phong City collectives.**

| Village | Farmer | Area cultivated m² | No. of ducks released/ 10a | Rice yield of duck fields kg/10a | Rice yield of conventional fields kg/10a | Value of rice from duck fields dong/10a | Value of rice from conventional fields dong/10a |
|---|---|---|---|---|---|---|---|
| A | 1 | 4000 | 100 | 400 | 400 | 5000 | 4200 |
| | 2 | 10,000 | 100 | 400 | 450 | 5000 | 4000 |
| | 3 | 3000 | 100 | 580 | 625 | 5500 | 4000 |
| | 4 | 5000 | 100 | 450 | 480 | 5500 | 4600 |
| | 5 | 10,000 | 100 | 400 | 420 | 5500 | 4600 |
| | 6 | 3000 | 80 | 400 | 430 | 5300 | 4300 |
| | 7 | 5000 | 100 | 249 | | 5300 | 4500 |
| | 8 | 20,000 | 100 | 450 | | 6800 | 6000 |
| | 9 | 2000 | 100 | 450 | 450 | 4500 | 3600 |
| | Avg. | 6,888 | 98 | 427 | 465 | 5,155 | 4,422 |
| B | 1 | 5000 | 50 | 500 | 550 | 4500 | 4500 |
| | 2 | 2800 | 40 | 600 | 650 | 4800 | 4800 |
| | 3 | 8000 | 60 | 600 | 630 | 4800 | 4800 |
| | Avg. | 5,266 | 50 | 567 | 606 | 4700 | 4700 |
| C | 1 | 3000 | 40 | 500 | 580 | 4500 | 4500 |
| | 2 | 2100 | 45 | 610 | 600 | 4600 | 4600 |
| | 3 | 2300 | 45 | 580 | 520 | 5000 | 5000 |
| | 4 | 2000 | 45 | 550 | 550 | 4800 | 4800 |
| | 5 | 1800 | 40 | 500 | 500 | 4800 | 4800 |
| | 6 | 3240 | 40 | 500 | 450 | 4500 | 4500 |
| | 7 | 2400 | 40 | 520 | 550 | 4800 | 4800 |
| | 8 | 3000 | 50 | 600 | 550 | 4700 | 4500 |
| | 9 | 5000 | 50 | 500 | 480 | 4500 | 4500 |
| | 10 | 3000 | 50 | 500 | 550 | 4500 | 4500 |
| | Avg. | 2,784 | 45 | 536 | 533 | 4,670 | 4,650 |

Notes:
A: Chien Thang Village, An Lao County, B: Quoc Tuan Village, An Duong County, C: Hoa Nghia Village, Kimanti County
Source: Prepared by the author from the 2006 questionnaire survey

Comparisons of yields in duck fields versus conventional fields in the same region are more important than comparisons of yields from IRDF in different regions. Such a comparison is shown in Table 5-6.

**Table 5-6. Yield ratios, price ratios and sales value ratios of collectives in Hai Phong City.**

|  | Yield Ratio | Price Ratio | Sales Value Ratio |
|---|---|---|---|
| Chien Thang Village | 0.91 | 1.16 | 0.89 |
| Quoc Tuan Village | 0.93 | 1.00 | 0.37 |
| Hoa Nghia Village | 1.00 | 1.00 | 0.35 |

Source: Prepared by the author from the 2006 questionnaire survey
Yield ratio = yield/10a of duck fields ÷ yield/10a of conventional fields
Price ratio = unit price of rice from duck fields ÷ unit price of rice from conventional fields
Sales value ratio = sales value of ducks produced/10a ÷ sales value of rice produced/10a

Yield ratio = yield/10a of duck fields ÷ yield/10a of conventional fields

In Chien Thang Village, 0.91

In Quoc Tuan Village, 0.93

In Hoa Nghia Village, 1.00

Only in Hoa Nghia Village was the yield obtained in duck fields and conventional fields the same, while in the other two villages, the yields from conventional fields were somewhat higher.

Price ratio = unit price of rice from duck fields ÷ unit price of rice from conventional fields

In Chien Thang Village, 1.16

In Quoc Tuan Village, 1.00

In Hoa Nghia Village, 1.00

Only in Chien Thang Village was the unit price of rice from duck fields higher than that from conventional fields.

The number of ducklings released per 10 ares was 98 in Chien Thang Village, 50 in Quoc Tuan Village, and 45 in Hoa Nghia Village, all ranging from between two to five times the number of ducks used in Japan.

This region is densely populated, with small per-household paddy field areas and poor yields. Moreover, as one can tell from the price ratios, because this is a developing country farmers are not always able to sell rice grown by IRDF at a higher price. This may be the reason why IRDF in this region has shifted more toward livestock breeding, as seen in the increased number of ducks released per unit area of paddy fields.

Table 5-6 shows the degree to which this shift has occurred.

Sales value ratio = sales value of ducks produced/10a ÷ sales value of rice produced/10a

In Chien Thang Village, 0.89

In Quoc Tuan Village, 0.37

In Hoa Nghia Village, 0.35

In Yanling Town, China, 0.11

In Anhui Province, China, 0.35

In South Korea, 0.018

This comparison shows clearly that the shift toward duck farming in IRDF has been due to economic factors.

**Figure 5-7. Characteristics of IRDF in northern Vietnam compared to that of Japan.**

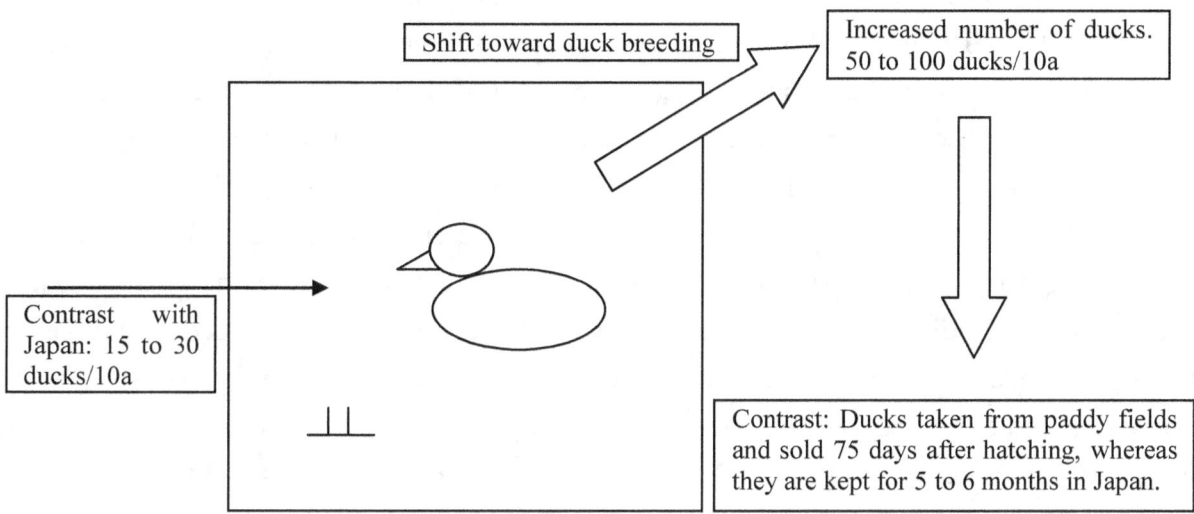

Source: Prepared by the author from the 2006 questionnaire survey

Figure 5-7 illustrates the shift toward livestock breeding in IRDF in northern Vietnam. The fattening period for domesticated ducks in Vietnam is about 75 days, after which they are taken from the paddy fields and immediately sold. In Japan, the *aigamo* ducks are raised for five to six months. I asked the Vietnamese why they sold them at 75 days. The answer was perfectly straightforward: "Even if we continue to feed them, the ducks do not grow any bigger after that." I have the feeling that if we tried to sell *aigamo* ducks in Japan at 75 days, no one would buy them because the taste would not be strong enough. This reflects differences between Japanese and Vietnamese food culture and shows the influence of Vietnam's rich duck-farming culture.

**5-8 Significance of the *Aigamo* Farmers' Exchanges in Asia**

Natural, socio-economic and historical conditions differ subtly among the various countries of Asia; Japan, China, South Korea, Vietnam, Cambodia, the Philippines, Malaysia, Indonesia, and so on. IRDF was developed in Japan and introduced into these countries with their different conditions, where it has developed further in diverse ways. The scale of the technique has been amplified in China, it has undergone collectivization in South Korea, and has shifted toward livestock breeding in Vietnam. Exchanges among duck farmers in Asia have also resulted in developments in the technology that would have been unimaginable in Japan alone.

Rice-field rats (*Rattus argentiventer*) live in the paddy fields of Vietnam. Rice-field rats are terrible pests that chew up the leaves of newly transplanted rice seedlings. Many Asian countries suffer damage from these pests. The International Rice Research Institute (IRRI) in Los Banos, Philippines has also tried stretching transparent plastic around the perimeters of experimental paddy fields to see if that would prevent the intrusion of rice-field rats.

The farmers in Hai Phong City discovered that the damage from these rats decreased very sharply in paddy fields occupied by ducks in IRDF. This is one more duck effect. The farmers in Thua Thien-Hue Province said the net around the paddy field perimeter was the reason. The farmers of Hai Phong City said the smell of the ducks' excrement kept the rats away. I therefore proposed spreading duck excrement only in a paddy field at the SAP Centre. The result was that damage from rice-field rats was sharply reduced. Practicing IRDF under the conditions that exist in the rest of Asia, quite different from those in Japan, makes it possible to carry out comparative experiments in ways not possible in Japan. Through comparison of the differences that emerge, IRDF can develop as a shared technology. This is the significance of the exchanges among duck farmers. Of course, exchange will also be important with other rice-farming regions such as Italy, Africa, Cuba and America. There are large differences between the methods of rice farming in these countries and those in Asia in terms of, for example, the scale of operations.

**Chapter 6**

**A Study of the Diffusion of Integrated Rice and Duck Farming (IRDF) in Asia in Terms of Farming System Theory**

In recent years, as we have seen in Chapters 4 and 5, IRDF has been spreading throughout many Asian countries, such as China, South Korea, Vietnam, and the Philippines. Why has this occurred? For example, if we compare what is happening in China with the situation in Japan, we can think of the following reasons.

1. Pollution of the environment

In China, vegetables, rice, soil, water, and so on, have been polluted due to excessive use of pesticides and chemical fertilizers. Because of this, IRDF has attracted wide interest as a farming method that can be carried out without the use of pesticides.

2. They already have ducks

As shown in Table 6-1, in 2002 there were 660 million (domesticated) ducks being raised in China and 60 million in Vietnam. In contrast to the Japanese, people in the rest of Asia are used to coming into contact with ducks on a daily basis. Because of this, they are easily able to enter the world of IRDF, simply as an extension of their daily life.

3. They are at an early stage of modernization

In Japan, farmers start to work with IRDF by giving up the use of 'convenient' herbicides, pesticides and chemical fertilizers, but in China, Vietnam and the Philippines the transplanting of rice seedlings and harvesting are carried out by hand, and in some places weeding is also carried out by hand. They are also used to keeping animals on a daily basis.

It is probably true to say that people in developing countries, who weed and transplant by hand and also keep livestock are able to start working on IRDF more easily than Japanese farmers who are now thoroughly used to enjoying the 'blessings of modernization.'

4. Understanding of the technique

Not a few Japanese people tend to think of 'IRDF' simply as a weeding technique. China, however, has a tradition of ecological farming practices, represented by 'duck paddy field grazing,' 'paddy field fish raising' and 'combined crop and fish culture' (*sang ji yu tang*).[27] Since they are able to compare IRDF with these practices, the Chinese have a more correct understanding of this technique, calling it "*dao-ya gongzuo*" (rice and ducks work together) while calling their traditional duck paddy field grazing "*daotian yangya.*"

5. Demand for ducks

China is the world's No.1 duck-consuming nation, Chinese people eat duck on a daily basis, and so there is a great demand for duck in China, which does not exist in Japan. Because of this, the ducks raised in the "*dao-ya gongzuo*" (rice and ducks work together) sell well.

---

[27] See Guo [129] for details of 'combined crop and fish culture' (*sang ji yu tang*).

6. Economic factors

Since in China rice produced through rice and duck farming fetches a good price, duck meat sells well, savings can be made on the costs of feed, and pesticide, herbicide and fertilizer costs are reduced or eliminated, the result is that incomes can be raised two or three times compared with conventional (modernized) rice farming.

7. State support and agricultural policies

The Chinese government provides subsidies for *aigamo* ducklings. Zhenjiang City (southern Jiangsu Province) pays a subsidy of 390 yen (about US$4) for each 10 ares of *aigamo* paddy field. This is a part of the 'No-pollution Food Action Plan' begun in 2001.

8. Economic growth

Shanghai City is achieving economic growth of nearly 10 percent per year. Ten percent of the population of 14 million people, 1.4 million people, have incomes roughly equivalent to the incomes of Japanese people. Because of this, there is a demand for 'duck rice,' mainly among people with high income levels.

As shown in Figure 6-1, it is said that era change occurs when all three elements of technology, values and institutions change. The reasons 1 to 8 given above mostly involve values and institutions.

So why has the 'IRDF' method introduced from Japan spread rather than the 'traditional duck paddy field grazing' they have always had? This is not an issue of values and institutions, but one of techniques, or technology. This chapter is a concrete comparative study of the differences in terms of techniques and farming system theory between Asian traditional duck paddy field grazing and IRDF from the perspective of the construction of the technique.

**Table 6-1. Current state of duck raising in Asia    (Millions of birds)**

|             | 1992  | 1999  | 2000  | 2001  | 2002  |
|-------------|-------|-------|-------|-------|-------|
| China       | 401.1 | 561.8 | 611.9 | 635.9 | 661.3 |
| Vietnam     | 37.3  | 53.8  | 54.5  | 57.0  | 60.0  |
| Philippines | 8.5   | 11.0  | 12.0  | 12.5  | 12.0  |
| Thailand    | 19.3  | 22.3  | 27.9  | 28.4  | 28.4  |
| South Korea | 1.0   | 4.3   | 5.4   | 6.7   | 8.0   |

Source: Prepared by the author from the FAO Corporate Document Repository, 2002

**Figure 6-1. The three factors involved in the changing of an era.**

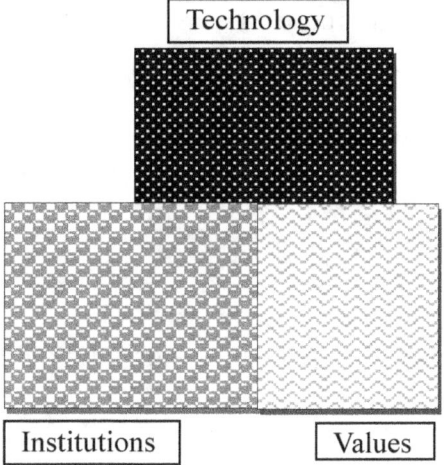

Source: Prepared by the author

## 6-1 Asian Peoples' Attitude of Acceptance for IRDF

**Figure 6-2. The process of diffusion of a technology**

Creation → Diffusion → Acceptance

Source: Prepared by the author

As shown in Figure 6-2, the process of diffusion of a technology has three stages, creation, diffusion and acceptance, but in the end acceptance by farmers determines everything.

How have Asian people who have handed down the technique of traditional duck paddy field grazing reacted to IRDF? I sent a survey (see Appendix) to *aigamo* practitioners in China, South Korea and the Philippines, asking them to write in their responses.

The survey asked, "Are there differences in the traditional (domesticated) duck paddy field grazing in your country and integrated rice and duck (*aigamo*) farming?" The following responses were received.

Jiangsu Province, China

1. There is no fence used in "*daotian yangya*" (duck paddy field grazing).

2. The ducks are released when the rice plants are in the middle (reproductive) growth phase.

3. The ducks are grazing in the paddy fields only for a short time.

4. The functions of integrated duck and rice farming are not seen.

Anhui Province, China

1. With IRDF we raise the ducks in the field 24 hours a day. In "*daotian yangya*" (duck paddy field grazing) we take the ducks to the paddy fields in the morning and release

them, and in the evening we take the ducks back to the sheds.

2. We do it for a different purpose. The purpose of carrying out IRDF is to stop using pesticides and chemical fertilizers. "*Daotian yangya*" (duck paddy field grazing) is simply for raising ducks.

3. IRDF has certain standards for the number of ducks and planting density of the rice plants. There are no such standards in "*daotian yangya*" (duck paddy field grazing).

South Korea

1. The important features of *orinongpop* (IRDF) are enclosing with a fence and making use of ecological diversity.

Vietnam

1. IRDF is scientific and carried out according to a plan.

2. In the traditional method, the ducks are the source of income. In IRDF, the rice fetches a good price and weeding labour is reduced.

3. In the traditional method the ducks were released into the fields after the rice harvest.

4. In the traditional method the ducks ate the paddy. In IRDF the ducks help *us*.

All of these different responses reflect the overall integrated and comprehensive nature of IRDF.

## 6-2 The Current State of Duck Raising in Asia

About how many ducks are being raised in Asian countries now? Table 6-1 was prepared based on FAO data. As can be seen from the data, with the exception of the Philippines in 2002, the number of ducks raised in all the Asian countries mentioned here rose in the ten-year period between 1992 and 2002.

## 6-3 The Relationship between Traditional Asian Duck Paddy Field Grazing and IRDF

As I have already mentioned in Chapter 4, pesticides and chemical fertilizers came to be used in China from the 1960s, and in Vietnam and the Philippines from the 1970s, causing the traditional duck paddy field grazing that had generally been carried out up until that time to decline dramatically.

However, as shown in Table 6-1, 661.3 million ducks were being raised in China, 60 million in Vietnam and 1.2 million in the Philippines in 2002. How were these ducks being raised? As far as I know and have experienced myself, almost all of them are being raised in sheds, including the use of semi-intensive shed methods. As mentioned previously, I have visited duck farms in many Asian countries, including China, Taiwan, Vietnam and the Philippines, and almost all of them were using semi-intensive shed methods. The ducks were being raised in sheds with a pond out in front and the area was structured so that the ducks could move freely between the shed and the pond. Large dogs were kept with the ducks in order to protect them.

Thus from the 1960s onwards, traditional Asian duck paddy field grazing declined dramatically, but duck raising itself did not come to an end and the raising of ducks continued in the form of intensive and semi-intensive shed raising methods. Since 1992, however, IRDF began to be introduced into Asia.

As indicated in Figure 6-3, an important point is that by the time IRDF was being introduced into Asia, almost all the duck raising had already switched over to shed-raising methods. It is certainly not the case that the traditional duck paddy field grazing was directly transformed into IRDF by paddy field enclosure.

**Figure 6-3. The relationship between traditional duck paddy field grazing and IRDF**

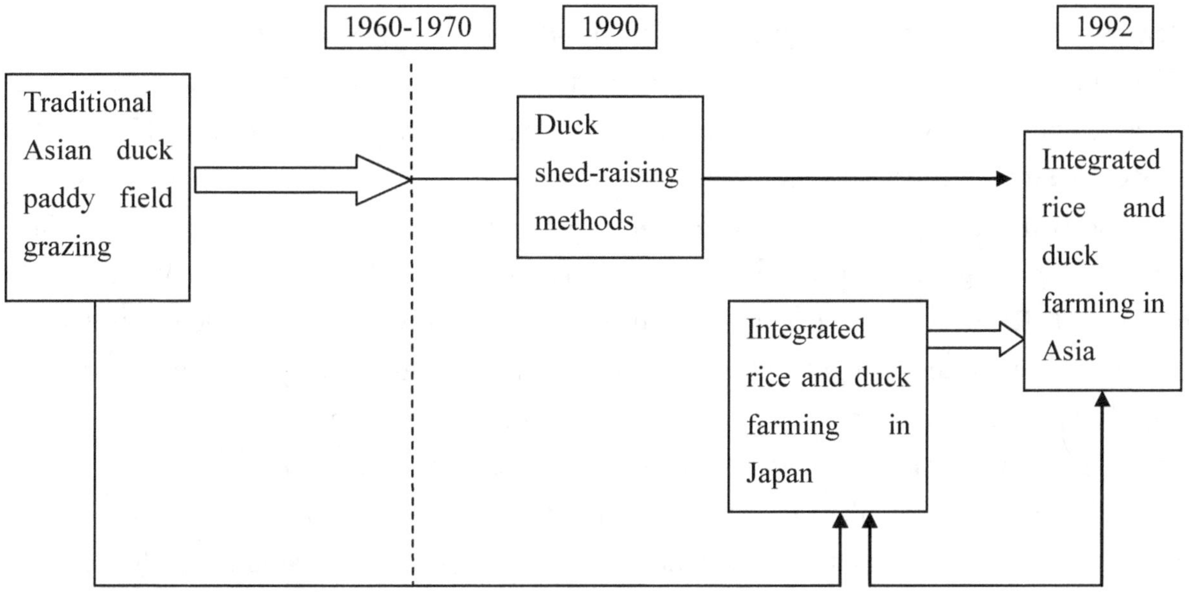

Source: Prepared by the author

In other words, the traditional duck paddy field grazing method was transformed into the shed-raising method and encountered the Japanese IRDF method from 1992 onwards, with characteristically Chinese developments. For example, the IRDF carried out in Jianhua Village, Longtang Township, Feisu County, Anhui Province that I mentioned in section 5-2 is a classic example. On 100 ha of rice farmers' paddy fields, three duck farmers set up fences around the fields and managed the raising of 30,000 ducks. This is a method that no one would think of in Japan, where there is no remnant of the traditional duck paddy field grazing method. This is precisely a rational fusion of Chinese waterfowl culture and Japanese IRDF.

The method used in Haiphong City, northern Vietnam, of releasing 50 to 100 ducks into each 10 ares of paddy field and selling the ducks after 75 days is also a rational fusion of Vietnamese tradition and IRDF that works within the local conditions.

If you think about it, taking an overall view, Japanese IRDF itself belongs to the genealogy of traditional Asian duck paddy field grazing. It is continuing to develop as it deepens exchanges with IRDF in Asian countries. Even though a certain traditional technique may have been introduced firstly from another country, it does not necessarily spread in exactly its original form. In many cases it will spread, be accepted and develop after additions of characteristic local innovations which help the method to adapt to the natural conditions of the accepting country. There are also cases where these innovations are transferred back to the original country. Thus it is that traditional techniques develop by repetition of creativity and imitation.

## 6-4 Enclosure is the Main Technical Difference between Traditional Duck Paddy Field Grazing and IRDF

As mentioned in Chapter 4, it was already known in China 700 years ago that ducks could perform insect pest and weed control and intertillage. This was also understood to some extent by the Vietnamese, Philippino, and Indonesian farmers.

Even in the rice production in the Mekong delta region, where direct sowing is carried out to a large extent, I have heard that they formerly released three-day-old ducklings into paddy fields on the third day after seedling transplantation in order to have them eat the insects.

In other words, people were to some degree aware of '*aigamo* effects' in traditional duck paddy field grazing. If we then compare the technology of traditional Asian duck paddy field grazing and IRDF on the basis of this premise, we eventually reach the conclusion that the difference between the two is 'enclosure.' It is also clear from the very diverse responses to the questionnaire mentioned in section 6-1 that IRDF begins with enclosure.

It is only after the field is enclosed as a limited space that such matters as the numbers of ducks released, their size, the period in the paddy field, the size of the rice seedlings, and so on, become realistic issues. These matters therefore almost never became issues that needed to be considered in the traditional Asian duck paddy field grazing, where the area of activity of the ducks is not limited or defined. Fattening the ducks was the main concern. The six *aigamo* effects on the rice plants become practical and effective through enclosure, which is the premise of each of these effects.

Even so, simply enclosing the traditional duck paddy field grazing would not automatically lead to IRDF. What is necessary is the viewpoint that sees rice cultivation and livestock in an integrated way and the creation of strategic technologies.

## 6.5 The Significance of Enclosure in Terms of Farming System Theory

As I have already mentioned in Chapter 3, in the European agricultural revolution arable land was enclosed with hedgerows and so on, the commons were abolished, privately-owned land was clearly demarcated, and the arable land was used intensively on the basis of the economic motivation of the pursuit of private profit.

Livestock were enclosed in sheds and were provided year-round with fodder grown on the arable land, the resulting manure being returned to the fields. Thus the arable land and the livestock were separately enclosed, and the cycle of fodder and manure was carried out through the medium of human labour.

On the other hand, in IRDF, as the rice and *aigamo* are simultaneously raised in a mutually beneficial way by enclosing them both within a paddy field, a system is created whereby the feed and the manure enclosed on the arable land are recycled through the animal power of the *aigamo*.

In the European agricultural revolution, weed prevention and control were established through innovations in the 'mechanical means of labour,' and achieved through the invention of the animal-powered row planter, animal-powered intertillage machinery, and the deep plough. The modernization of agriculture was built up on the basis of progress in this system of the means of labour.

In contrast, was 'an innovation in the means of labour' carried out in IRDF? In the sense that a creative use of the energy of animal power of the *aigamo* has substituted for the manual labour of humans, we can certainly say that an 'animal-powered means of labour' innovation has taken place. Since I was weeding by hand, I felt this very strongly during the ten years before I discovered *aigamo*. It was an innovation involving the shift from manual labour to animal power.

Thus, the definitive feature of IRDF is enclosure, but the theoretical significance of this enclosure becomes clear when we focus on the 'container-like means of labour' as one of the component factors of agricultural productivity.

In his book, *An Introduction to Agricultural Management*, Professor Iso-o Iwakata writes about the features of the container-like means of labour as follows: "Here I will examine the container-like means of labour. Land, especially arable land, is a place for raising crops and livestock. Crops are exposed to warmth and provided with water. Further, facilities such as livestock sheds, silkworm-rearing rooms and greenhouses protect crops and animals from wind and rain, aid in the adjustment of temperature and humidity, and mainly contribute to improvements in productivity through physical and chemical manipulation. In that sense, there is no difference between these and mechanical means of labour. What is different is that the latter, mechanical means of labour, contribute directly and positively to productivity improvements through dynamic manipulation, whereas the role of the former, container-like means of labour, is in many cases indirect and supplementary." [7]

In light of the features of the container-like means of labour, the enclosure of IRDF is indeed nothing less than an innovative creation arising from the container-like means of labour concept. In IRDF, the container-like means of labour, the limited area of the paddy field, make possible and supplement the energetic activities of the *aigamo* as the 'animal-powered means of labour' through the act of enclosure The traditional Asian duck paddy field grazing system also made use of the animal-powered means of labour, but lacking the 'container-like means of labour' of the enclosed paddy field did not come to combine the 'container-like means of labour' into the system as a component factor of productivity. Put another way, in terms of historical continuity, the 'container-like means of labour' was indispensible for traditional Asian duck paddy field grazing to become 'integrated' in the true sense of the word.

We can say that the livestock sheds of the European agricultural revolution were precisely a 'container-like means of labour' which made possible and supplemented the system of reproduction of fertility expansion.

The difference between the Asian IRDF and the European agricultural revolution is based on whether the crops and livestock are enclosed in a 'container-like means of labour' simultaneously in the same space or are enclosed separately.

Figure 6-4 is a diagrammatic representation of the component factors of agricultural productivity. It can be seen that, at the same time as the innovations of the animal-powered means of labour and the container-like means of labour are indispensable in IRDF, understanding rice cultivation and livestock in a unified way and making strategic use of human labour are necessary.

Nevertheless, although in the usual agricultural technology humans are 'used' as a means of labour to work upon the object of labour, by 'deploying' *aigamo*, the animal-powered means of labour, in the enclosure, the container-like means of labour, in IRDF, rice and *aigamo* are raised together, thereby exhibiting the *aigamo* effects in a natural and timely fashion without the need for humans to 'use' or 'manage' each of the components separately.

## 6-6. The Goals of Enclosure

When considering, in the first place, why the paddy field is enclosed, the following three reasons can be mentioned.

1. To prevent the *aigamo* from escaping from the paddy field.
2. To prevent predators from invading the paddy field.
3. To raise the level of the *aigamo* effects for the rice plants.

These three goals are not independent of each other, since only by having *aigamo* not escape from the paddy field and by not having predators invade the enclosure, do we at last reap the benefit of the cause and effect relationship of the enhancing of the *aigamo* effects for the rice plants.

If it were just for achieving the goal of ensuring that the *aigamo* or domesticated ducks did not escape from the paddy field, a simple fence would be sufficient. In countries which have a very long history of raising ducks, such as China, Vietnam, the Philippines, a certain degree of balance and loss dispersal has been established between humans, ducks, and predators such as dogs. Compared with Japan and South Korea, it seems that losses due to predators are far lower in these large duck-raising countries. One problem that is more serious than predators is thieves. In this case, the ducks are kept in a shed by the house or someone has to stand guard over the paddy field during the night. In these countries, the fences enclosing the paddy fields are simple and made of diverse materials such as palm leaves, bamboo, branches of trees, nets, and so on.

On the other hand, in countries where few ducks are raised and people do not come into contact with ducks on a daily basis, such as Japan and South Korea, predator attacks are a huge problem. No balance has been established in the relationship between humans, *aigamo* and predators and thus, electric fences are necessary to protect against predators in Japan. In South Korea, a simple net fence is erected around the paddy field and the *aigamo* are kept in a strong metal shed at night. Thus, there is a great difference in the forms that enclosures take in different countries.

**Figure 6.4 Component Factors of Agricultural Productivity**

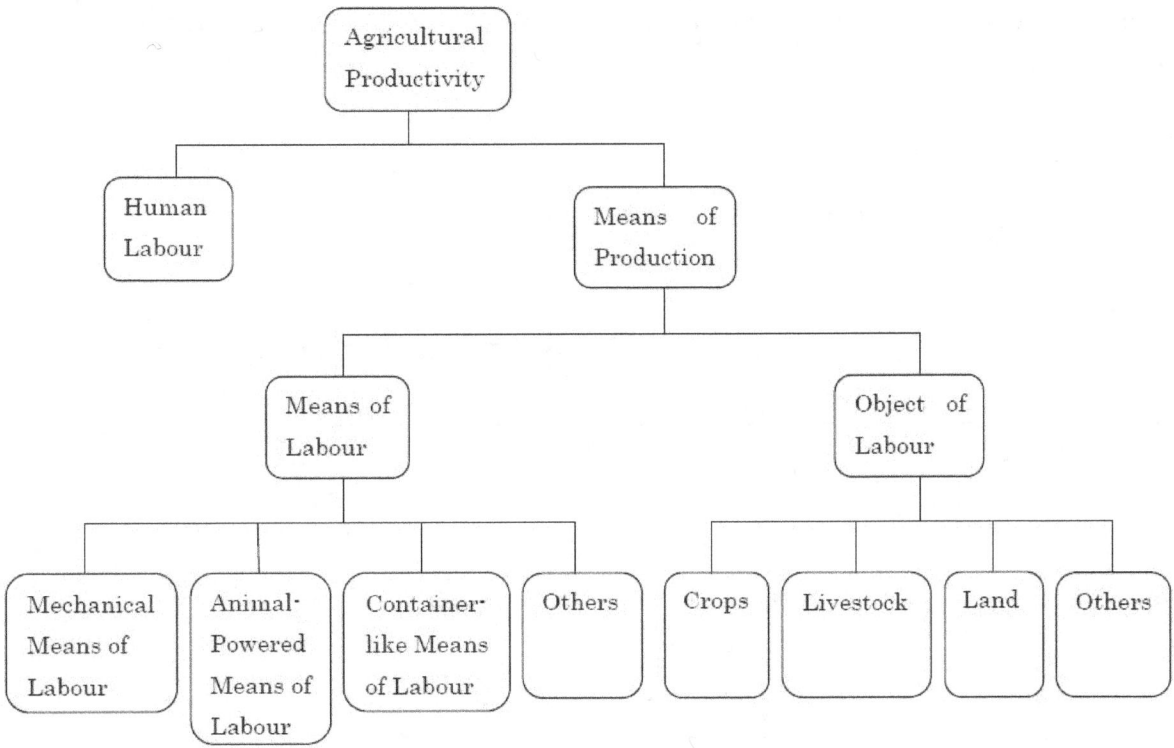

Source: Based on Masao Tsuji, *Considering Asia's Agricultural Modernization*, p.36, [30], with revisions by the author.

## 6-7 Enclosures and the Behaviour of *Aigamo* and Domesticated Ducks

Interestingly, the behaviour of *aigamo* and domesticated ducks depends upon whether or not there is an enclosure. When I saw domesticated ducks released into a paddy field with no enclosure in Vietnam, I noticed something very interesting. Perhaps it was because the muscles, skeleton and feathers of the ducklings were in the developmental stage, but the ducklings far preferred to eat the protein of insects than to eat the weeds. In search of tasty food, while pecking at the leaves and the bases of the clumps of rice plants, the ducks clambered over the small levees between paddy fields and, as shown in Figure 6-5, moved about horizontally from paddy field to paddy field.

In contrast, in enclosed paddy fields where IRDF is carried out, at first, just as domesticated ducks graze freely in the traditional Asian method, the *aigamo* go around the paddy field horizontally eating their favourite insects that have alighted on the corrugated plastic sheet (for protecting the levees) surrounding the paddy field or are sitting on the rice plant leaves. Next they eat weeds and seeds that are floating on the water or weeds that are growing under the water. Lastly, they push their beaks into the mud and eat the tubificid worms that live in the mud and the weeds and weed seeds that come floating up.

In other words, in the limited space of IRDF, the *aigamo* move vertically at the same time as they move horizontally, as shown in Figure 6-6. Because of this three-dimensional pattern of movement, the *aigamo* effects on the rice plants are manifested continuously, comprehensively, homogenously and in a timely fashion.

Below is a stylized form of the different movements of the behaviour patterns of *aigamo* with and without enclosures.

**Figure 6-5. *Aigamo* movements when there is no enclosure**

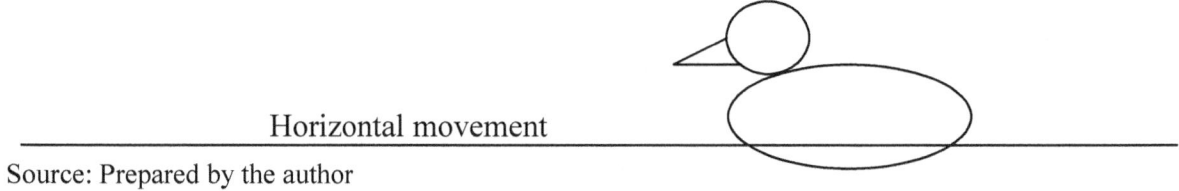

Source: Prepared by the author

**Figure 6-6. *Aigamo* movements when there is an enclosure**

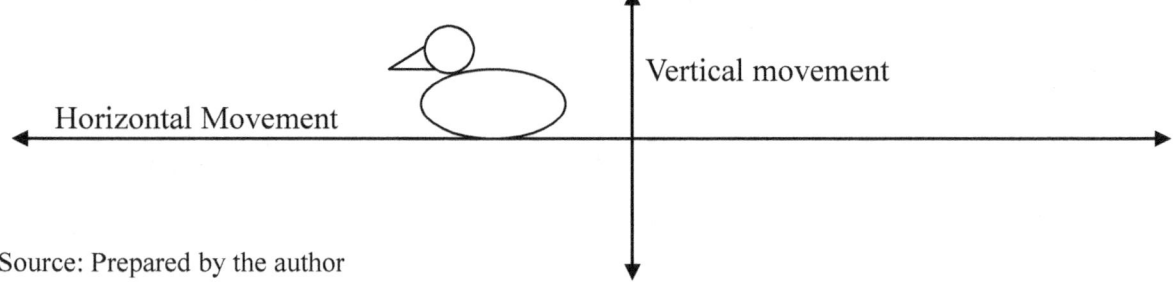

Source: Prepared by the author

In traditional duck paddy field grazing, where there is no enclosure, since there will be various kinds of paddy fields with their various conditions in the area, the ducks will prefer to go to the paddy fields that have deep water, plentiful feed, and which are safe, and so it is not necessarily the case that the ducks will cruise around all of the fields in the area in a uniform fashion. Take for example the paddy field A in Figure 6-7. Even if the owner of paddy field A releases ducks into his paddy field, if there is plentiful feed to be found in field F, the ducks will all gravitate towards field F and since there is no enclosure around field A the activities of the ducks cannot be limited to that field. Thus there is no guarantee of the uniformity of the *aigamo* effects.

**Figure 6-7. Duck behaviour when paddy fields have no enclosure**

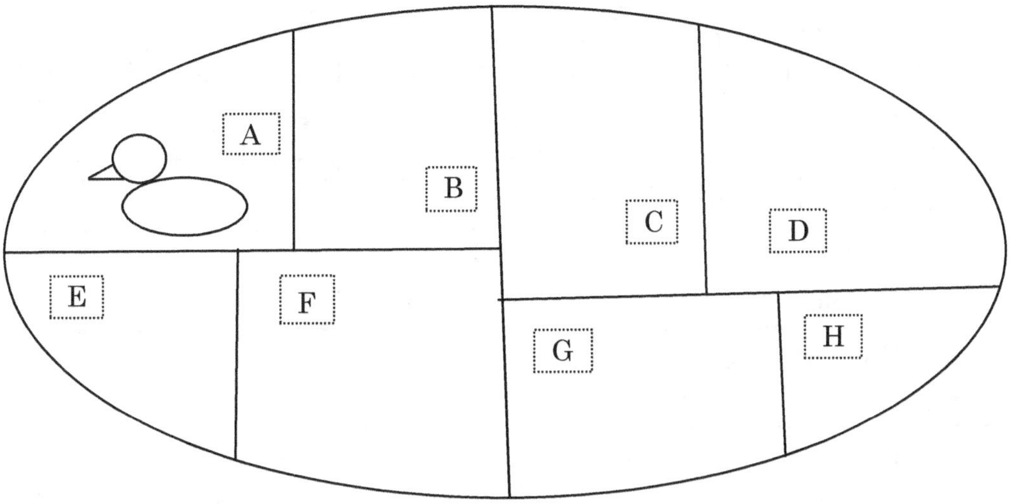

Source: Prepared by the author

## 6-8. *Aigamo* Effects are Enhanced by Enclosure

In this section we examine concretely, from the point of view of principles, how the presence or absence of enclosures influences the mechanism of IRDF for each of the six *aigamo* effects on the rice plant that were explained in Chapter 2.

## 6-8-(1) Weed suppression and control

The weed suppression and control effect of IRDF is quite obvious from the contents of Table 6-2.

In IRDF, the most pernicious weed is *hie* – 'barnyard millet' or 'Japanese millet' (*Echinochloa esculenta*). *Hie* is also a member of rice plant family (Poaceae) and so *aigamo* do not eat it. However, IRDF makes possible an almost perfect suppression of *hie*. As shown in Figure 6-8, this is because *aigamo* eat the *hie* seeds, cause the sprouted *hie* seeds to float to the surface of the water by stirring them up with their beaks and feet, or bury and trample the seeds deeply into the mud. As shown in Figure 6-9, this can only be done within the first two weeks after the transplanting of rice seedlings, when the *hie* is at a growth stage where the roots are not yet extensive and entrenched.

**Table 6-2. A comparison of the *aigamo* weed control effect**

| | | Hie, Japanese millet | Konagi, Monochoria vaginalis (var. plantaginea) | Azena, Lindernia procumbens (Krock) Borbas | Kikashigusa, Rotala indica var. uliginosa | Kayatsurigusa, Cyperaceae | Mizohakobe, Elatine triandra | Abunome Dopatrium junceum | Himemisohagi, Ammannia multiflora | Total |
|---|---|---|---|---|---|---|---|---|---|---|
| *Aigamo* plot | Number | 1 | 1 | 2 | 7 | 3 | Some | - | - | - |
| | Air-dried weight | 0.1 | t | t | 0.1 | t | t | - | - | 0.2 |
| No-weeding plot | Number | 8 | 102 | 4 | 10 | 4 | Some | 2 | 4 | - |
| | Air-dried weight | 9.8 | 49.2 | 0.6 | 1.5 | 0.3 | 2.3 | t | t | 57.4 |
| Hand-weeded plot | Number | - | 102 | 4 | 10 | 4 | Some | - | - | - |
| | Air-dried weight | - | 13.4 | 0.1 | 0.2 | 0.1 | 0.1 | - | - | 13.8 |

Notes: 1) "Number" is the number of plants/m$^2$, Air-dried weight is in g/m$^2$

2) "t" means less than 0.05 g

3) All three plots were areas of the same paddy field that were partitioned off with nets.

4) Survey conducted on July 31, 1994

Source: Takao Furuno, IRDF Expanding Toward Infinity, p.33. [43]

Figure 6-9 shows the stages of the growth of *hie*. As you can see, when *hie* has put out three or more leaves the roots are already spreading deeply into the mud and the plant does not easily float to the surface even if the *aigamo* are stirring up the soil. *Hie* reaches the three-leaf stage about two weeks (12-15 days) after seedling transplantation. This is the basis for releasing *aigamo* into the paddy field within two weeks after transplantation.

In an enclosed paddy field, the *aigamo* are moving around the whole field and the water in the field is always muddy. In duck paddy field grazing with no enclosure, however, even if *aigamo* are released into the fields within two weeks after transplantation, as shown in Figure 6-7, there is no guarantee that the *aigamo* will go around the intended paddy fields in a uniform manner. Thus, in the absence of enclosure 'timeliness' cannot be secured and therefore weed prevention and control,[28] especially the effect against *hie*, will be reduced in traditional duck paddy field grazing. Let us look at an example from China.

---

[28] See Kusahina [23] and Miyahara [85] for further thinking on weed prevention and control.

**Figure 6-8. The mechanism of *aigamo* weed prevention and control**

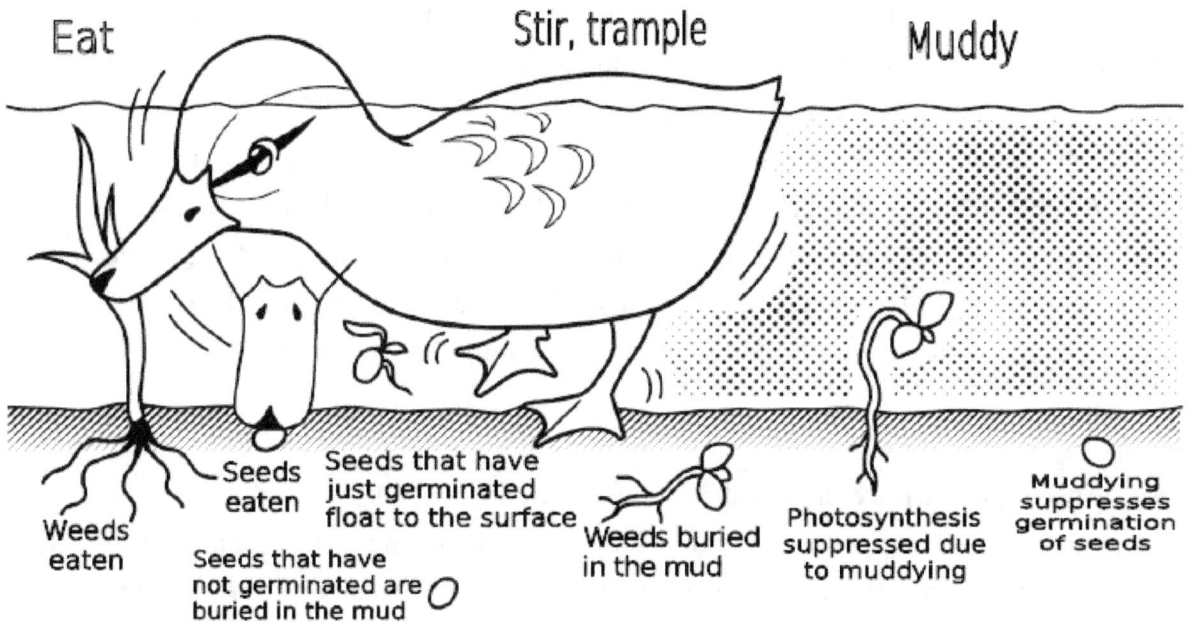

Source: Takao Furuno, IRDF Expanding Toward Infinity, p.33. [43]

**Figure 6-9. Growth of *hie* and timing of release of *aigamo***

Aigamo released before this point

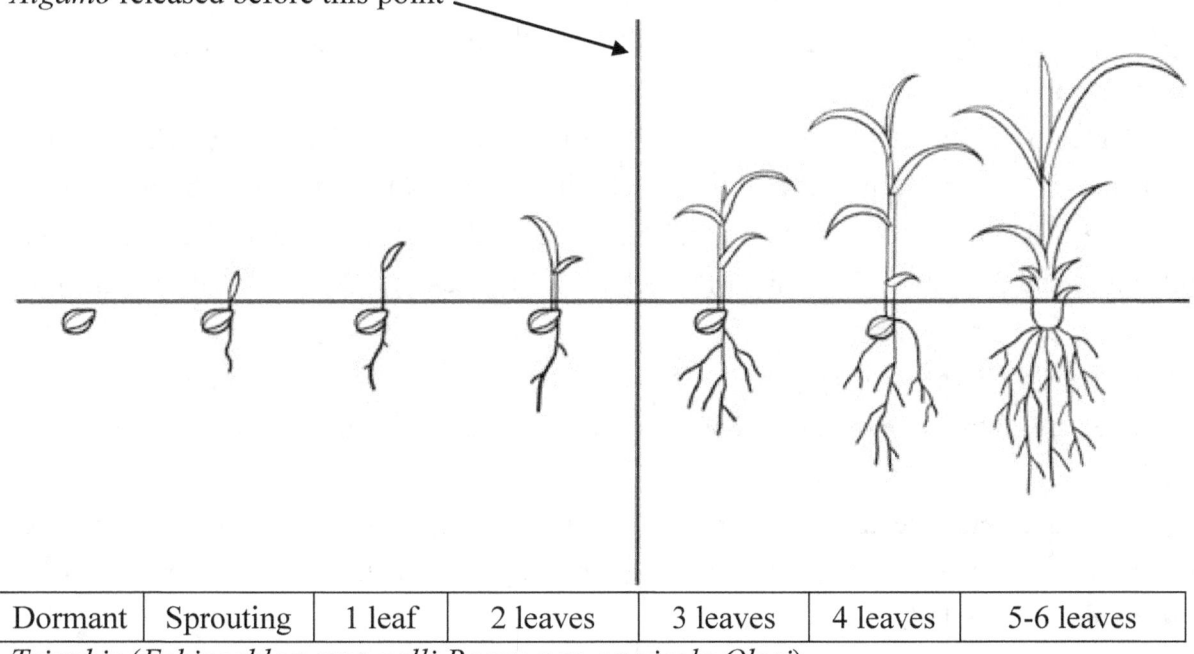

| Dormant | Sprouting | 1 leaf | 2 leaves | 3 leaves | 4 leaves | 5-6 leaves |
|---------|-----------|--------|----------|----------|----------|------------|

*Tainubie (Echinochloa crus-galli Beauv. var. oryzicola Ohwi)*
Approximate standard growth (after seedling transplantation)
3-4 days after transplantation: 0.5 leaves, 7-10 days after transplantation: 1-1.5 leaves
12-15 days after transplantation: 2.0-3.0 leaves
Source: This figure is a diagram of the growth of *hie* drawn by the Agricultural Produce Research Department of the Fukuoka Agricultural Research Centre to which the author has added information concerning the timing of *aigamo* release.

"Duck raising insect protection (*yangya fangchong*) not only protects rice plants from insect pests, a great amount of weeds are also eaten. The ducks also provide intertillage. In the fields into which ducks were released, the field was fine with just one intertilling for the first crop. The fields into which ducks had not been released required a second intertilling." [97]

This short quotation tells us exactly what the possibilities and limitations are for intertillage weed control in traditional duck paddy field grazing with no enclosure.

In integrated rice and duck culture, usually not even one round of intertillage weed control by human labour is required. I think you can see quite clearly the difference in weed prevention and control in enclosed and unenclosed paddy fields.

### 6-8-(2) Insect pest suppression and control

In general, surprisingly little attention has been paid to the excellent ability of birds in insect pest suppression and control in agriculture. This is because birds are free to fly in the skies and are active over great distances in contrast to spiders, which are fairly stationary within fields.

Regarding this point, in IRDF it is possible to limit the range of activity of *aigamo* by enclosing the paddy field, and thus enclosure has opened up the path for the use of birds as natural predators. Table 6-3 shows the effect of *aigamo* grazing on the establishment of migratory planthoppers. The excellent ability of *aigamo* in insect pest suppression and control is quite plain.

In September 2005, the whole of Kyushu was affected by a large outbreak of brown planthoppers. The area affected by patches of withered rice plants was 400 ha in Fukuoka Prefecture, 2,000 ha in Kumamoto Prefecture, 140 ha in Nagasaki Prefecture, 280 ha in Oita Prefecture, and 337 ha in Kagoshima Prefecture. In this case, IRDF exhibited its full insect pest suppression and control effect.

"I am the only farmer carrying out IRDF in my hamlet and it was only in my paddy fields that there was no loss due to planthoppers. All the fields around mine suffered from withered patches."

I received letters like these praising the insect pest suppression and control ability of *aigamo* from all over Kyushu. 2005 threw the insect pest suppression and control ability of *aigamo* into sharp relief.

**Table 6-3. Effect of *aigamo* grazing on the establishment of migratory planthoppers**

| Test plot | *Tobiirounka*[a] (Insects per 25 hills) | *Sejirounka*[b] (Insects per 25 hills) | Gonosomatic index |
|---|---|---|---|
| *Aigamo* plot | 0 | 6 | 9.3 |
| Sparsely planted *aigamo* plot | 0 | 2 | 2.7 |
| No-weeding plot* | 4 | 260 | 100.0 |
| No-weeding sparsely planted plot* | 0 | 98 | 53.3 |
| Hand-weeded plot* | 6 | 314 | 98.7 |
| Conventionally farmed plot* | 2 | 12 | 24.0 |

Notes: * Control plots

The gonosomatic index (GI) is calculated according to the following equation:

GI = (1 × I + II × 2 + III × 3) / (3 × 25) × 100

I: Gonosomes seen on 1/3 of the whole stem

II: Gonosomes seen on 1/3 to 2/3 of the whole stem

III: Gonosomes seen on 2/3 or more of the whole stem

a: Brown planthopper, a group of planthoppers, *fulgoroidea*

b: Whitebacked planthopper, *Sogatella furcifera* Horváth

Source: Survey by the Project Team of the Fukuoka Agricultural Research Centre.

Planthoppers,[29] the most serious insect pest threat to rice in Japan, generally migrate from China and Southeast Asia in late June and early July. They lay their eggs approximately three or four days after arrival and then increase as shown in Figure 6-10. (From Kunihiko Naba, *Planthoppers*, Rural Culture Association Japan, p.80)

In IRDF, the planthoppers fly in, but are not allowed to lay their eggs because they are caught and eaten by the *aigamo* before they can do so. Since *aigamo* do not eat planthopper eggs, the *aigamo* must be released and 'stationed' in the paddy fields before the planthoppers arrive. The *aigamo* then capture and eat the planthoppers, maintaining planthopper density at a low level. Thus damage does not occur.

As planthoppers hatch from the eggs and their density increases, and as the number of stems of the rice plant increases it becomes more difficult to discover planthopper infestation.

It is really important from the point of view of the 'timeliness' of insect pest suppression and control to have the *aigamo* 'stationed' in the paddy fields before the planthoppers fly in over the sea. In the unenclosed traditional duck paddy field grazing system it may be difficult to attain the 'timeliness' of insect pest suppression and control. This is because, since there is no enclosure, the *aigamo* are not 'stationed' in a certain limited space. In IRDF, *aigamo* are released into the paddy fields within two weeks after seedling transplantation. As transplantation is generally carried out in May or early June, the *aigamo* are already 'stationed' in the paddy fields when the planthoppers fly in from China and Southeast Asia in late June to early June.

Thus the 'timeliness' required for insect pest control is secured by IRDF, where there are always a fixed number of *aigamo* in a certain space of paddy field.

---

[29] See Furuno [46] for more information on planthoppers.

**Figure 6-10. Mechanism of planthopper suppression and control by *aigamo***

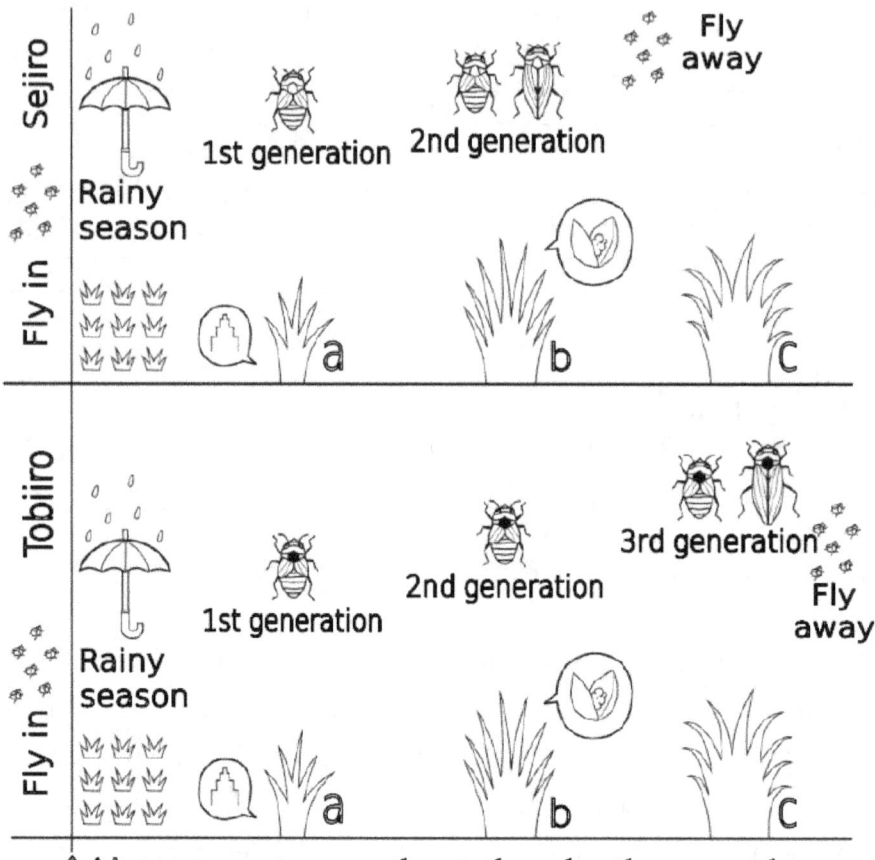

↑Aigamo capture and eat the planthoppers here

Notes: a: young panicle formation stage, b: young panicle stage, c: mature stage

Source: Kunihiko Naba, *Planthoppers*, with additions by the author. [34]

## 6-8-(3) Nutrient provision effect

### 6-8-(3)-a The Mechanism of 'Homogeneity'

As shown in Figure 6-11, raising *aigamo* in a paddy field filled appropriately with water, *aigamo* droppings instantly form a suspension in the water. In addition, as the *aigamo* paddle the water, everything is stirred up and widely dispersed. Furthermore, as can be seen from Table 6-4, with 20 birds in 10 ares, the amount of faeces produced per day is about 3 kg (189 ÷ 60). A little of the faeces falls into the water and is dispersed every day. The result of this is that in an *aigamo* paddy field filled with water the nutrient is provided in an extremely homogenous fashion.

It is also interesting to note that the droppings of cattle, sheep, and chickens on pasture are in solid form and have no dispersal mechanism such as that seen in IRDF.

By enclosing a paddy field, the *aigamo* act uniformly over the whole area of the field. In traditional duck paddy field grazing, where there is no enclosure, the ducks move from one paddy field to the next and this 'homogeneity' becomes structurally impossible.

**Table 6-4. Fertilizer content of *aigamo* faeces**

| (1) Fertilizer effect per bird (during two months' grazing in the paddy field) (Unit: g) | | | |
|---|---|---|---|
| Amount of faeces | Nitrogen | Phosphate | Potassium |
| 9,457 | 47 | 70 | 31 |
| (2) Fertilizer effect per 10 ares (20 birds) (Unit: kg) | | | |
| | Amount of faeces | Nitrogen | Phosphate | Potassium |
| *Aigamo* faeces | 189 | 0.94 | 1.40 | 0.60 |
| Standard fertilizer amounts | | 6.00 | 6.00 | 6.00 |
| Sufficiency | | 16% | 23% | 10% |

Source: Analytical Data from Kagoshima University Faculty of Agriculture Fertilizer Science Research Laboratory, 1994

**Figure 6-11. The mechanism of dispersion of *aigamo* faeces**

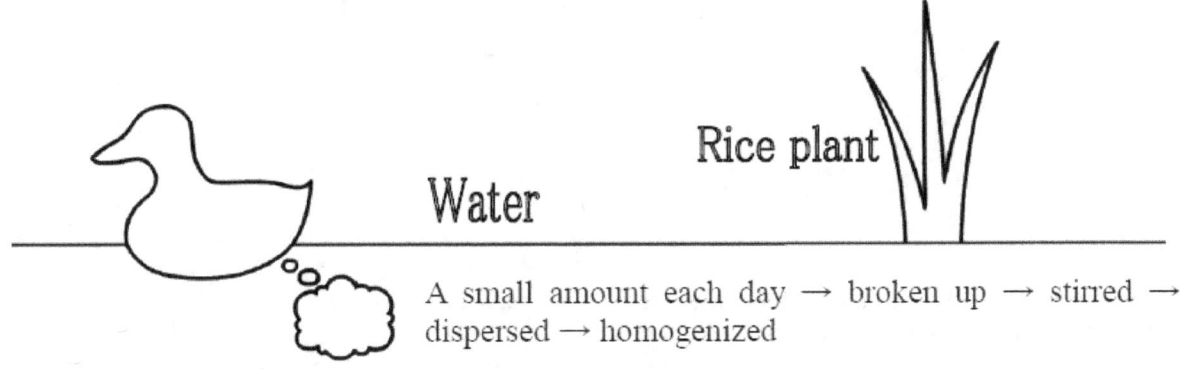

A small amount each day → broken up → stirred → dispersed → homogenized

Source: Prepared by the author

## 6-8-(3)-b The premise of sustainability

Professor Kazuhiko Egashira of the Soil Science Laboratory of Kyushu University examined the nitrogen content of the soil of *aigamo* paddy fields to which no fertilizer had been added for five years. Figure 6-12 shows one part of the results. It can be seen that there was a regular pattern where total nitrogen in the *aigamo* field increased in the period May to October, when IRDF was carried out, in 1997, 1998, and 1999, and decreased in the in the off-season from October to May.

In contrast, the conventionally farmed fields, which used a total of 6 to 7 kg/10 ares of chemical fertilizer as basal dressing and after-manuring, showed almost no change over the year.

**Figure 6-12. Annual changes in total soil nitrogen content in integrated rice and duck paddy fields** Unit: g/kg

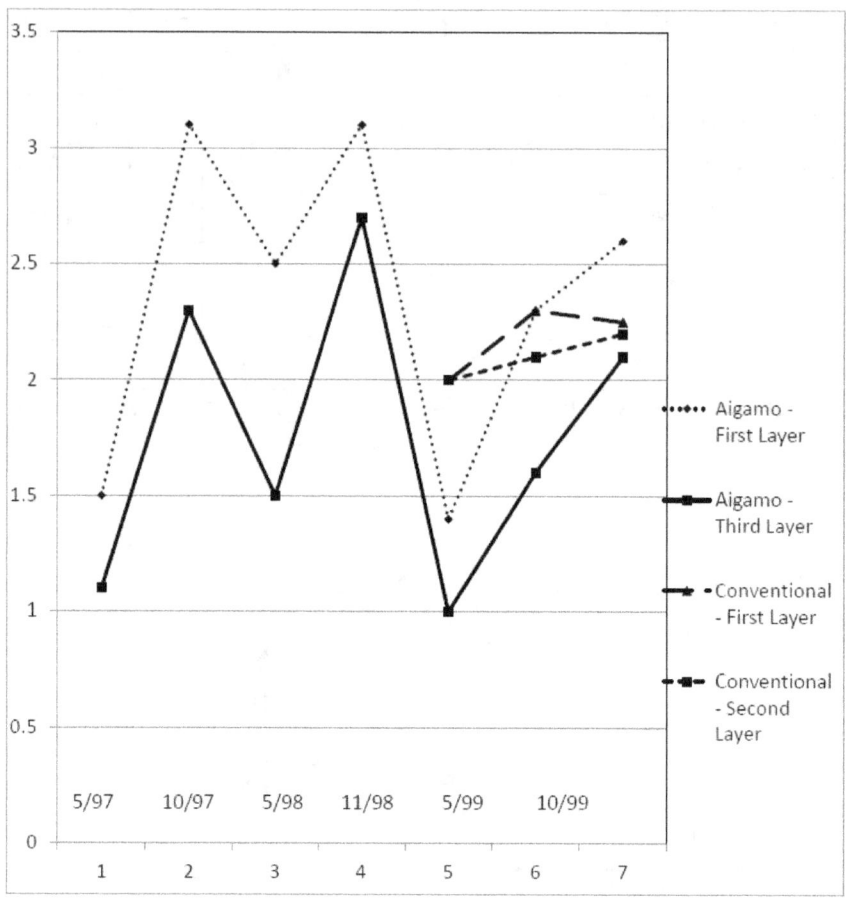

*Aigamo* paddy field layers: First: 0-4.5 cm, Second: 4.5-6 cm, Third 6-17 cm
*Conventional paddy field layers: First: 0-5 cm, Second: 5-12 cm
*Measurements were taken before seedling transplantation (before fertilizer application in the conventional field) in May and following the harvest in October.

Source: Kazuhiko Egashira, Yoshiyuki Inoue, Fumiaki Tajima, Faculty of Agriculture, Kyushu University, [10]

This unfertilized field produced a harvest of nearly 500 kg of *genmai* (brown rice) per 10 ares by IRDF. However, as shown in Table 6-4, the nitrogen provided by *aigamo* droppings in the *aigamo* paddy field was a mere 0.9 kg. Despite the fact that total nitrogen should have increased in the conventionally farmed paddy field, to which 6 to 7 kg of nitrogen were input, for some reason total nitrogen *did* indeed increase in the *aigamo* paddy field, in which only a little less than one kilogram of nitrogen was 'input' from *aigamo* droppings. It is still uncertain where this nitrogen has come from.

This phenomenon is one which appears when the paddy field is enclosed and a fixed number of *aigamo* are released into the field for a certain period of time.

The total nitrogen content throughout the whole soil is higher after the harvest has been completed than after the seedling transplantation was completed. We can say that this hints at the 'basis of sustainability' of IRDF.

Even now there are some aspects of the mechanism[30] of nutrient (mainly nitrogen) provision of *aigamo* paddy fields that are not well understood.


**6-8-(4) Stimulation effect**

Figures 6-13 and 6-14 are from the research carried out by Gao Shengda of The United Graduate School of Agricultural Sciences of Kagoshima University. Figure 6-13 shows that the shape of the rice plants becomes short and thick from the stimulus effect of the *aigamo*. Figure 6-14 clearly shows how the number of rice plant stems increase from the same stimulus effect. Group behaviour of the *aigamo* in the paddy field results in *aigamo* constantly brushing up against the rice plants, giving them continual stimulus. This is not simply stimulus given by the pecking of the base of the clumps with their beaks. The *aigamo* brush up against the rice plants with their whole body. They give physical stimulus to the above-ground part of the rice plant by striking the leaves with their wings when they spread their wings while swimming, by eating insects which have settled on the leaves, and by pushing their heads into the rice plant clumps. At the same time, they also give physical stimulus to the roots below the ground with their beaks and feet. According to Yasuo Ohta, this *aigamo* contact stimulus generates a plant hormone, ethylene, which results in the unique shape of the rice plant. Giving stimulation to rice plants in a large field by human labour is an immense task, but *aigamo* released into a paddy field carry out this task automatically. This is an effect that arises through the combination of the two qualitatively differing elements of a plant and an animal. This is an area in which *aigamo* are superior to any other method.


**Figure 6-13.　Changes in the height of rice plant stems in experimental paddy fields**

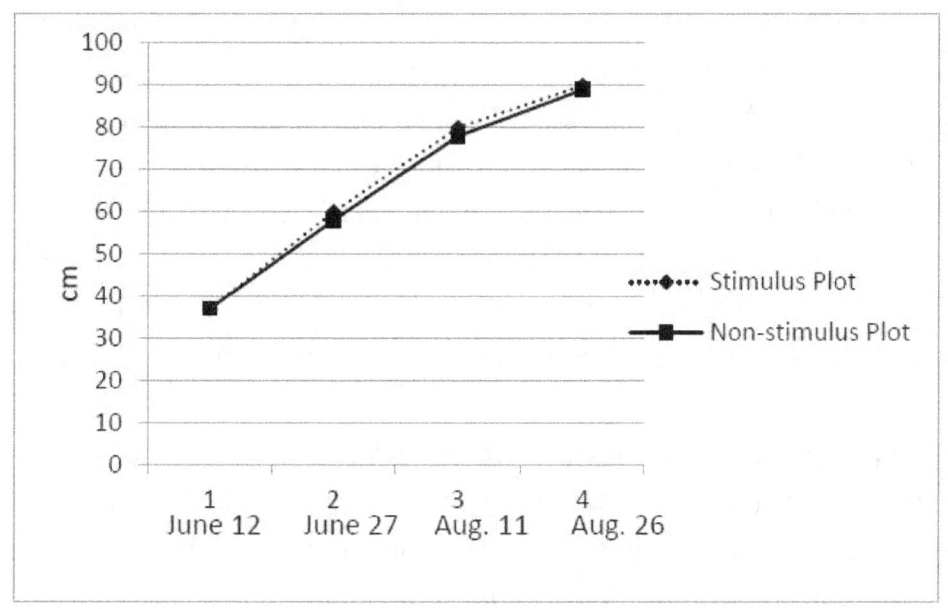

Source: Kagoshima University Faculty of Agriculture

---

[30] See Furuno [58] for more on the nitrogen cycle in *aigamo* paddy fields.

**Figure 6-14. Changes in rice plant stem numbers in experimental paddy fields**

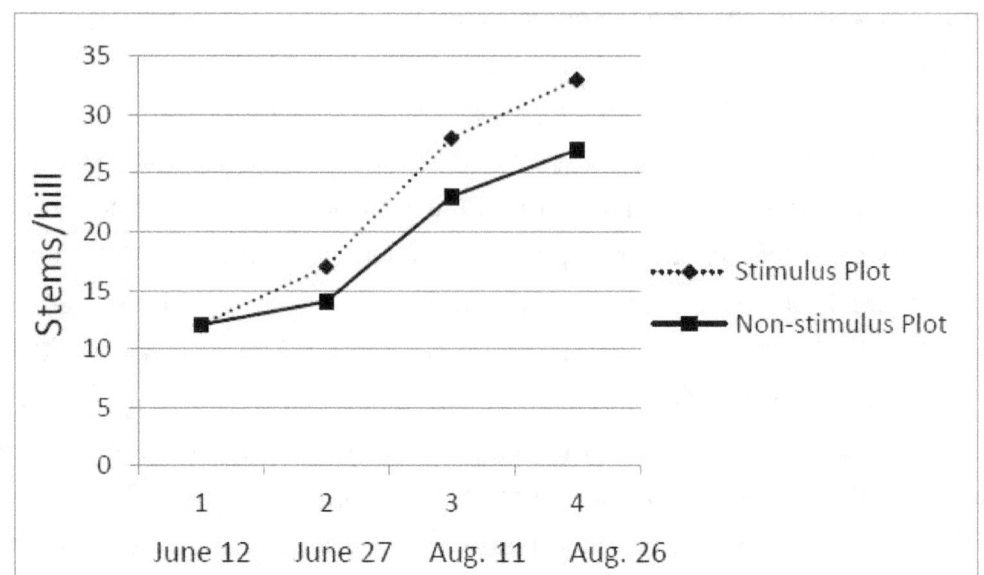

Source: Kagoshima University Faculty of Agriculture

It is indeed this stimulus effect that can only arise when the paddy field is enclosed to form a limited space in which the *aigamo* graze. It is unreasonable to expect that this effect would occur by releasing domesticated ducks into an unenclosed paddy field, as in the traditional Asian duck paddy field grazing method. This is therefore truly an effect that has been brought about through enclosure.

I have already explained about the stimulus effect in detail in Chapter 2. The *aigamo* rice paddy shows marvellous rice plant growth characteristics. Deep green, think and wide leaves that pierce the sky, thick stems, plentiful in number, and an overall short and thick shape. This is due to the stimulus effect of the *aigamo* constantly giving contact stimulus to the rice plants both above and below ground.

In order to manifest this effect and achieve this marvellous *aigamo* rice plant form effectively, the *aigamo* stimulus effect[31] is necessary right from the early stages. Unless the *aigamo* stimulus effect is given in a timely manner, the number of stems will not increase.

This stimulus effect is one aspect of IRDF that will only demonstrate its full effectiveness in an enclosed paddy field. The effect cannot be expected to appear in traditional Asian duck paddy field grazing, where *aigamo* are allowed to move freely from one field to the next.

### 6-8-(5) The full-time ploughing and muddying effect (the F effect)

When *aigamo* are released into an enclosed paddy field, they move their beaks and feet vigorously, moving about and engaging in feeding behaviour. The whole surface of the field soon becomes a muddy brown colour. In IRDF, for the two to three months during which the *aigamo* are released into the paddy field, the water is always muddy.

---

[31] See Furuno [77] for more on the stimulus effect.

The result of this is that the soil of the paddy field becomes soft like a caramel pudding. After the harvest in the autumn, if you dig into the soil in an *aigamo* paddy field with a spade you will see a fine three-layered structure, such as that shown in Figure 6-15. The soil in a control field will not show this three-layered structure.

**Figure 6-15. Soil structure in an *aigamo* field**

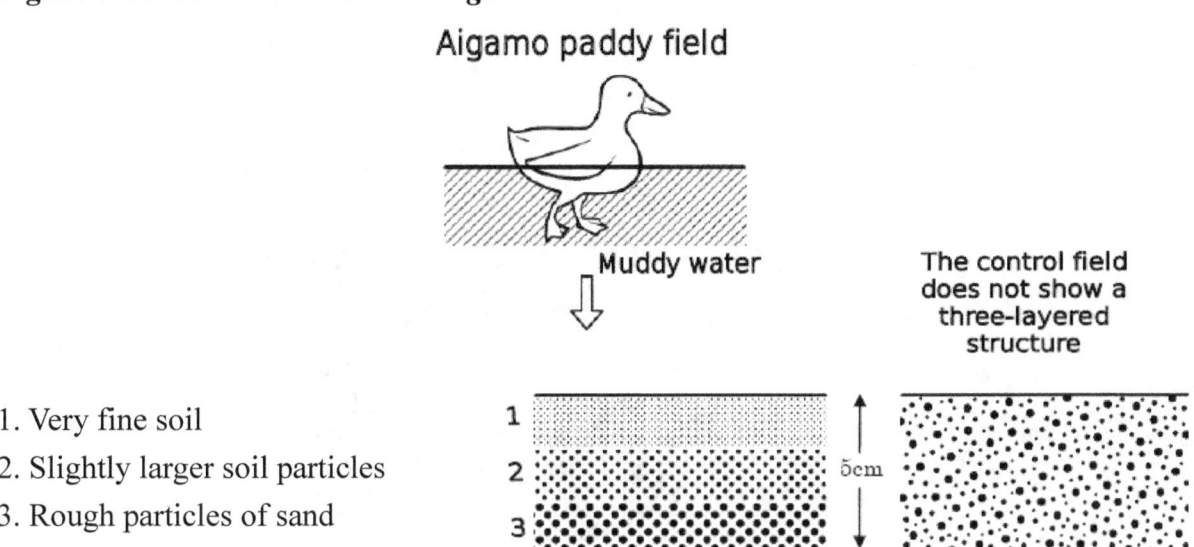

1. Very fine soil
2. Slightly larger soil particles
3. Rough particles of sand

Source: Takao Furuno, *Aigamo Banzai*, p.47. [44]

When this soil structure appears in an *aigamo* field, water retention improves markedly. This is especially effective in intermediate and mountainous areas where there are many stones in the plough pan and water retention is poor. In contrast, *aigamo* fields dry out easily after water has been released from the field. This is because large cracks appear in the surface layer of fine particles after water has been drained off, thus improving the vertical permeability of water. At the same time, this is aided by the fact that grooves appear in the soil surface where the *aigamo* have passed between the rows of rice plants, helping the surface water to run off quickly. This full-time ploughing and muddying F effect is one that arises only when *aigamo* are active in a limited space, and is unlikely to occur in traditional Asian duck paddy field grazing. This is because as the ducks move to another field the water in the field they have just moved out of will soon become clear again.

*Aigamo* paddy fields retain water well when they are filled with water and dry quickly when the water is drained off. This F effect is one that only occurs when *aigamo* are released into a limited space, continuous muddying being impossible in Asian duck grazing, where ducks are permitted to move around freely from one paddy field to the next.

### 6-8-(6) The golden snail control effect

Just after the *aigamo* ducklings have been released into the paddy field, their beaks are small and they feast on the small golden snails that have just hatched from eggs. As the *aigamo* grow and their beaks become larger, they start to eat the larger golden snails.

The *aigamo* is the greatest natural predator of golden snails in Japanese paddy fields. The *aigamo* control effect on golden snails is clear from Figure 6-16.

**Figure 6-16.** ***Aigamo* control effect on golden snails** (September 6, 1991 survey)

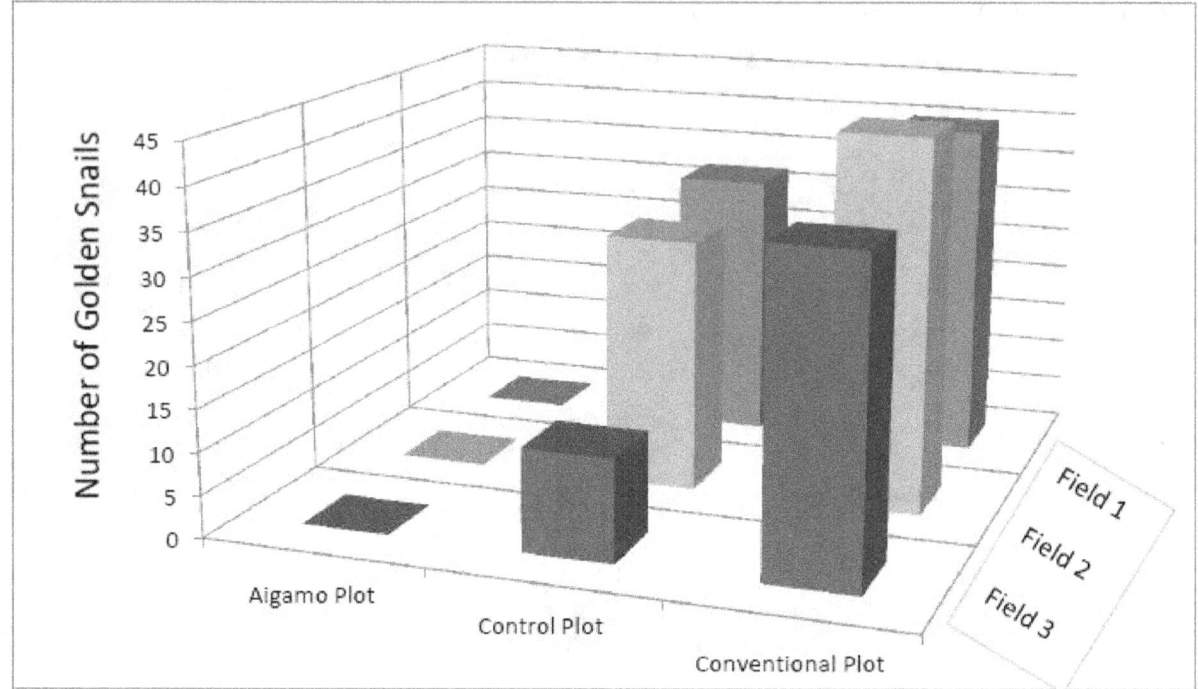

Note: Area of each plot: 120 cm × 120 cm
Source: Professor Masaharu Manda, Kagoshima University

In fact golden snails are edible and in Vietnam are one of the ingredients used in a rice noodle dish called *pho*. I have eaten them several times, but cannot say that I find them very tasty. When *aigamo* eat golden snails they turn into very palatable duck meat. Golden snails are not consumed in Japan and thus the *aigamo* make effective use of a formerly unused resource.

This effect is also one that becomes very conspicuous when the paddy field is enclosed.

## 6-9 Super System

Compared with the unenclosed traditional Asian duck paddy field grazing, the enclosed IRDF system shows extremely high levels of effectiveness in weed control, insect pest control, stimulation, full-time ploughing and muddying, and golden snail control carried out with good timeliness, homogeneity and sustainability, as has been shown with reference to the principles of IRDF mechanisms. It is probably fair to say that enclosure has given rise to effects that did not originally exist rather than say that enclosure heightened the expression of the effects.

As I have already mentioned in Chapter 2, it is not the case that humans exert detailed management and control over these *aigamo* effects. IRDF is not a technique in which large numbers of ducks are taken to the paddy field because weeds and insect pests have appeared, as shown in the "Illustration of ducks raised to control locusts" in Chapter 4. By raising rice and *aigamo* simultaneously right from the beginning, the six *aigamo* effects appear together in a natural and timely manner as a result of raising the rice and the *aigamo* together freely. This is an important point.

I call this a 'super system' in the sense that the six effects appear in a timely and natural manner without any direct management of the *aigamo* effects by humans. I use the word 'super' to show clearly the relationship between 'enclosure' and the holistic integrity of the *aigamo* effects.

One beginner rice farmer commented, "IRDF is a method that is easily taken on by someone who is facing the challenges of rice farming for the first time. You simply release the *aigamo* into the paddy field, and the *aigamo* and the rice grow up by themselves. Detailed management is not necessary." It is indeed this super system, the total system whereby the rice and the ducks grow up by themselves, that is the greatest effect brought about by enclosure of the paddy field. This super system concept would simply not result from non-enclosed traditional duck paddy field grazing.

## 6-10 Various Conditions Requiring Enclosure

Whether or not it was true in the 1950s, releasing *aigamo* into paddy fields in present-day Japan is impossible without enclosing the field with a net or electric fence. The *aigamo* would immediately invade the surrounding fields, which would be unforgivable. Even if it were allowed, some of the *aigamo* might die from the pesticides sprayed on the crops from time to time. Thus, in the present as in the past, when releasing *aigamo* into the paddy fields there is no other method but to enclose one's own field.

Because of this, rather than having enclosed the paddy fields due to prior knowledge of the *aigamo* effects, by enclosing the fields and limiting the range of the activities of the *aigamo*, notions such as the right number of *aigamo* and the timing of release began to arise, and as a result the *aigamo* effects became more vividly apparent.

In the monsoon areas of Asia, livestock were originally not kept in sheds and provided with feed, but were put out to graze. Animals such as ducks, chicken, pigs and water buffalo were put out to graze on pasture, in ponds, rivers and post-harvest fields during the day, eating natural feed that did not compete with human food, and kept in sheds at night. That was the main method of Asian livestock breeding.

However, even in the Asian countries where this tradition existed, the use of large amounts of pesticides and chemical fertilizers became the norm with the modernization of agriculture. The result of this has been that traditional duck paddy field grazing has become difficult in China, Vietnam and Indonesia, where ducks have now come to be raised in sheds. This traditional duck paddy field grazing has been passed on in a developed form in IRDF, where surrounding the paddy field with a fence prevents the problems that arise from pesticide use.

Looked at as an historical continuum, we may consider that were two choices for traditional Asian duck paddy field grazing (Figure 6-17).

(1) Modernization in which livestock breeding specializes only in duck raising.

(2) A method by which inheritance of the tradition of duck paddy field grazing bonds rice cultivation more deeply with livestock breeding through enclosure.

This represents a 'modern Asian revival of traditional duck paddy field grazing.'

A fully-fledged rice cultivation technology only becomes possible through the 'evolution' of traditional Asian duck paddy field grazing to IRDF. Thus it has become a 'technology' through which a certain degree of effect on the rice plants can be expected by anyone decides to try to implement it.

**Figure 6-17. Two patterns of Asian duck grazing**

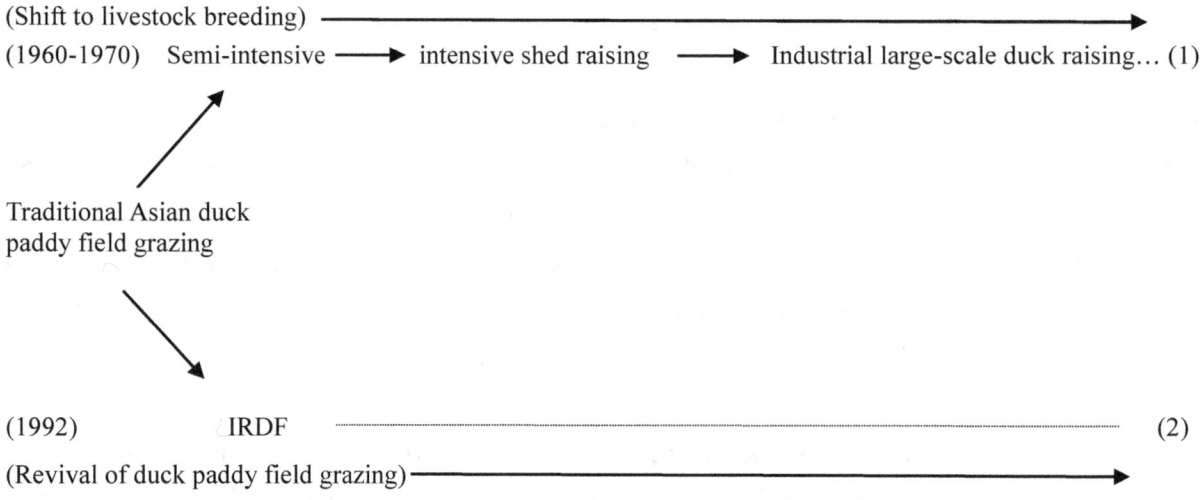

Source: Prepared by the author

## 6-11 Management Evaluation of IRDF

Since the main viewpoint of this chapter focuses on 'enclosure,' I have thus far discussed the 'technological rationality' of IRDF. In order for a technology to spread, however, 'economic rationality' as well as technological rationality is necessary. Although the discussion of economic rationality is not the main theme of this paper, in the sense of complementing the study of technological rationality, I will give a management evaluation of IRDF here. The data below is 'management content evaluation' carried out by Kagoshima University as a research case study.

## Table 6-5. Labour input per 10 ares in rice cultivation (Unit: minutes/10 ares)

| Task | Conventional farming | | | Aigamo farming | | |
|---|---|---|---|---|---|---|
| | Average | Standard Deviation | Coefficient of Variance (%) | Average | Standard Deviation | Coefficient of Variance (%) |
| Autumn Ploughing | 109.1 | 76.9 | 71 | 180.0 | 123.2 | 68 |
| Fertilizer spreading | 126.7 | 192.3 | 152 | 105.2 | 210.0 | 200 |
| Dry coarse ploughing | 239.1 | 239.0 | 123 | 324.5 | 342.9 | 106 |
| Seed sowing | 133.3 | 110.2 | 83 | 99.8 | 112.9 | 113 |
| Watering after seed sowing | 151.2 | 143.7 | 95 | 131.7 | 171.3 | 130 |
| Basal dressing | 79.2 | 66.3 | 84 | 84.3 | 62.0 | 74 |
| Puddling and levelling | 106.1 | 59.1 | 56 | 133.3 | 48.2 | 36 |
| Seedling transplantation | 250.9 | 220.6 | 88 | 297.2 | 277.7 | 93 |
| Herbicide spraying | 19.1 | 16.2 | 85 | 0.0 | 0.0 | - |
| Hand weeding | 266.7 | 444.8 | 167 | 466.7 | 580.6 | 124 |
| Pest/weed control | 0.0 | 0.0 | - | 0.0 | 0.0 | - |
| Top dressing | 39.0 | 55.4 | 142 | 10.0 | 34.6 | 346 |
| Levee management | 172.8 | 408.6 | 236 | 265.5 | 503.6 | 190 |
| Water management | 300.7 | 281.6 | 94 | 482.1 | 376.3 | 78 |
| Harvest | 244.8 | 313.6 | 128 | 179.1 | 164.6 | 92 |
| Drying | 122.6 | 323.7 | 264 | 184.5 | 402.2 | 218 |
| Shipping | 30.2 | 102.2 | 338 | 49.0 | 127.6 | 260 |
| TOTAL | 2391.4 | 1433.6 | 60 | 2992.8 | 1415.2 | 47 |
| TOTAL (Hours) | 39.9 | 23.9 | 60 | 49.9 | 23.6 | 47 |

## Table 6-6. Main expenditures per 10 ares in rice cultivation (Unit: yen/10 ares)

| Expenses | Conventional farming | | | Aigamo farming | | |
|---|---|---|---|---|---|---|
| | Average | Standard Deviation | Coefficient of Variance (%) | Average | Standard Deviation | Coefficient of Variance (%) |
| Basal dressing | 5,160 | 2,229 | 43 | 5,219 | 3,457 | 66 |
| Seeds | 3,466 | 6,052 | 175 | 1,658 | 1,896 | 114 |
| Seedling trays | 5,639 | 7,021 | 125 | 7,139 | 7,751 | 106 |
| Top dressing | 1,590 | 2,069 | 130 | 80 | 266 | 332 |
| Watering after seed sowing | 1,933 | 1,374 | 71 | 0 | 0 | - |
| Pest/weed control | 1,902 | 664 | 35 | 209 | 693 | 332 |
| Depreciation | 62,556 | 44,651 | 71 | 46,545 | 31,863 | 68 |
| Labour | 24,715 | 15,220 | 62 | 30,404 | 15,222 | 50 |
| Other | 15,851 | 12,474 | 79 | 16,273 | 14,449 | 89 |
| TOTAL | 122,812 | 46,193 | 38 | 107,528 | 31,430 | 29 |

## Table 6-7. Rice yield and profit from sales

| | Conventional farming | Aigamo farming |
|---|---|---|
| Yield (kg/10 ares) | 468 | 455 |
| Total harvest (kg) | 5,255 | 3,852 |
| Marketed volume [30 kg bag] | 121 | 122 |
| Marketed volume (kg) | 3,622 | 3,651 |
| Marketed proportion (%) | 69 | 95 |
| Unit price [yen/30 kg] | 9,135 | 14,192 |
| Gross income (yen/10 ares) | 139,030 | 210,679 |
| Total sales (yen) | 1,190,423 | 1,751,944 |

Note: Since figures are averages over a number of farms values are not calculable within the table.

## Table 6-8. Time used for *aigamo* rearing and care (Unit: minutes/10 ares)

| | Average |
|---|---|
| Care of *aigamo* before releasing into paddy field | 240.4 |
| Setting up nets, poles and electric fence | 411.2 |
| *Aigamo* grazing | 23.2 |
| Providing *aigamo* feed | 303.9 |
| *Aigamo* patrol | 64.6 |
| *Aigamo* capturing | 41.1 |
| TOTAL | 1,084.4 |
| TOTAL (hours) | 18.1 |

## Table 6-9. *Aigamo* rearing and care expenses (Unit: yen/10 ares)

| | Average |
|---|---|
| *Aigamo* ducklings | 4,969.3 |
| *Aigamo* feed | 5,984.6 |
| Nets, poles and fencing | 10,217.6 |
| TOTAL | 21,171.5 |

## Table 6-10. Farming income and net profit (Unit: yen/10 ares)

| | Conventional | Aigamo | Derived from |
|---|---|---|---|
| Gross farming income (A) | 139,030 | 210,679 | Table 6-7, sale of rice. |
| Rice cultivation expenses (B) | 98,097 | 77,124 | Table 6-6 Total - Labour Cost. |
| *Aigamo* expenses (C) | - | 22,202 | Table 6-9. See note 3. |
| Farming income (D) [(A)-(B)-(C)] | 40,933 | 111,353 | |
| Rice cultivation labour expenses (E) | 24,715 | 30,404 | Table 6-6. |
| *Aigamo* labour expenses (F) | - | 11,858 | Table 6-8. |
| **Net farming income [(D)-(E)-(F)]** | **16,218** | **69,091** | |

Notes:
1) The tables above are quoted from a graduation paper by Keiichiro Kuru, written under the guidance of Professor Izumi Iwamoto at the Faculty of Agriculture, Kagoshima University. Note that sales of *aigamo* meat are not included. The data in Table 6-10 is derived from Tables 6-5, 6-6, 6-7, 6-8 and 6-9.
2) Subjects of the survey for the graduation paper were eight conventional farmers and twelve *aigamo* farmers in Koyama Town, Kimotsuki County, Kagoshima Prefecture. All figures in the tables are averages of the surveyed farmers. The survey was carried out between mid-November and December 2000. The survey methodology was a fact-finding survey carried out by interviews with individual subjects.
3) Aigamo expenses given here (22,202 yen) differ from the figure given in Table 6-9 (21,171.5 yen) because the rice cultivation expenses of one farmer in the *aigamo* group were not investigated in the survey. The figure in Table 6-9 is the average of the whole group and the figure given here is the average of the farmers in the group after the one farmer is excluded.
4) Labour expenses are calculated from hourly rates related to food and beverage manufacturing in Miyazaki Prefecture in 1998 and work out at something over 600 yen/hr.

(1) Gross income is the average of gross income for all farms.

Gross income for conventional farming = 139,030 yen

Gross income from *aigamo* farming = 210,679 yen

(2) Farming income = gross farming income – (direct expenses + depreciation)

Farming income from conventional farming

= Gross farming income – rice cultivation expenses

= 139,030 – 98,097 = 40,933 yen

Farming income from *aigamo* farming

= Gross farming income – (rice cultivation expenses + *aigamo* expenses)

= 210,679 – (77,123 + 22,202) = 111,354 yen

(3) Net farming income = Farming income – labour expenses

Net farming income for conventional farming = farming income – labour expenses for rice cultivation

= 40,933 – 24,715 = 16,218 yen

Net farming income for *aigamo* farming = farming income – (labour expenses for rice cultivation +*aigamo* labour expenses)

= 111,353 – (30,404 + 11,858) = 69,091 yen

Concerning the above survey results, the author stated, "It is indicated that although there is some demerit in terms of management expenses and hours of labour input compared to conventional farming the merit in gross farming income sufficiently compensates for this. Sales of *aigamo* are not included in the income comparison. The farming income is extremely high even if this income from the sale of *aigamo* is ignored, which is quite a remarkable result."

Moreover, although an academic study of the Furuno farm IRDF has not been carried out, based on experience thus far the Furuno farm management anticipates a yield in 2007 of 500 kg/10 ares, equal to the average yield for the region, and a unit price of 500 yen/kg, which has been stable for 30 years.

| | |
|---|---|
| Farmed area | 4.2 ha |
| Yield | 500 kg/10 ares |
| Unit price | 500 yen/ kg |
| Selling price of *aigamo* meat | 2,500 to 3,000 yen/bird |
| Number of birds used | 20 to 30 birds/10 ares |

● Gross income

| | |
|---|---|
| Gross income from rice | 500 yen/kg $\times$ 500 kg = 250,000 yen |
| Gross income from *aigamo* meat | 3,000 yen/bird $\times$ 20 = 60,000 yen |
| TOTAL | 310,000 yen |

● Expenses

| | |
|---|---|
| *Aigamo* ducklings | 500 yen $\times$ 20 = 10,000 yen |

However, since the farm is self-sufficient in ducklings the cost is almost zero.

| | |
|---|---|
| *Aigamo* processing | - 1000 yen/bird |
| Thus the processing cost per 10 ares is: | 1,000 yen/bird $\times$ 20 birds = 20,000 yen |
| Feed | Since almost all the feed is rice screenings mixed with gravel received free of charge from the rice mill, the cost is close to zero. |

● Labour expenses: Not calculated, but is thought to have been reduced due to labour saving in work relating to the electric fence, estimated at about 40% of the labour expenses.

Table 6-11 is an example from Vietnam. We can see from the table that although, in general, rice produced by IRDF does not necessarily sell for a higher price than rice produced by other methods in developing countries in Asia, because of savings made on the relatively expensive chemical fertilizers, pesticides and labour costs for weeding, and the fact that the ducks can be sold, incomes for IRDF are higher than those for conventional farming. As far as I can judge from what I have seen and heard, it can be considered that economic rationality is secured in both developed and developing countries in Asia.

The spread of IRDF in Asia in recent years is most likely a reflection of this economic rationality.

Moreover, although the focus of this paper is on a comparative study of the technical aspects of farming system theory, the importance of a study of the management aspects, which also require study, has once again been brought to my attention. I therefore intend to undertake a business management analysis of the Furuno Farm.

**Table 6-11. Income-expenditure comparison of *aigamo* farming and conventional farming in Vietnam**

| Item | Calculation | *Aigamo* farming | Conventional farming |
|------|-------------|------------------|----------------------|
| **Expenses** | | | |
| Seeds and seedlings | 3 kg × 3,000 | 9,000 | 9,000 |
| Ploughing (labour) | 3 cap × 10,000 | 30,000 | 30,000 |
| Seedling transplantation (labour) | 1.5 cap × 10,000 | 15,000 | 15,000 |
| Compost | 200 kg × 150 | 30,000 | 30,000 |
| Phosphate fertilizer | 10 kg × 1,000 | 10,000 | 10,000 |
| Nitrogen fertilizer | 5 kg × 3,000 | | 15,000 |
| Weeding (labour) | 2 cap × 10,000 | | 20,000 |
| Pesticides | | | 15,000 |
| *Aigamo* | 15 birds × 2,500 | 37,500 | |
| Feed | 2.5 kg × 15 birds × 2,000 | 75,000 | |
| Fencing | 120,000 ÷ 6 seasons | 20,000 | |
| Total Expenses (A) | | 226,500 | 144,000 |
| **Income** | | | |
| Yield (*aigamo*) | 150 kg × 2,000 | 300,000 | |
| Yield (conventional) | 130 kg × 2,000 | | 260,000 |
| *Aigamo* meat | 14 kg × 13,000 | 182,000 | |
| Total income (B) | | 482,000 | 260,000 |
| **Balance (B-A)** | | 255,000 | 116,000 |

Source: Prepared by Director Tran Van Nhu, SAP Centre
Notes: Units: Area, 1 *sao* = 360 m$^2$, currency, 1 dong = 0.01 yen)

## 6-12 Labour saving: A Technical Problem of IRDF

I will discuss here the labour saving brought about by the latest techniques in the direct sowing of *aigamo* paddy fields that I am now developing, and the enclosure of paddy fields. It was while pursuing the labour-saving technology of direct sowing of *aigamo* paddy fields (integrated rice and duck culture + dry-paddy direct sowing) that the ideas for labour saving in the work of enclosure came about.

### 6-12-(1) Organic farming vs. efficiency

Overexertion in the pursuit of efficiency has caused modernized agriculture to use large amounts of pesticides, herbicides and chemical fertilizers, has made agriculture reliant upon machinery, and has brought about a wide array of problems and issues such as environmental destruction, the overuse of energy resources, and food safety.

On the other hand, organic farming results in the production of very palatable and safe farm produce, but since it uses no pesticides, herbicides and chemical fertilizers, meticulous attention must be paid to the crops, insect pests and weeds, and this is very labour intensive.

This is a very commonsense understanding of modernized farming and organic farming. At least, looking at the current situation, this seems to be correct. However, organic farming and efficiency are not necessarily opposed concepts, and things might change if technological conditions alter.

From my 30-year experience of organic farming, greater efficiency and labour saving in organic farming are always practical issues on the farm.

For practical organic farming work, the following three methods are available:

1) Large inputs of human labour

2) Mechanization

3) Innovation

Method 1) increases human labour input to carry out the work by employing workers.

Method 2) is a suitable form of mechanization for organic farming, such as mechanical weeding.

Method 3) rethinks the whole technological system. Greater labour saving and efficiency in organic farming is the subject of 2) and 3). The discussion concerning labour saving by *aigamo* direct sowing and enclosures is a rethinking of the whole technological system.

### 6-12-(2) *Aigamo* direct sowing – another form of IRDF

As shown in Figure 6-18, world rice cultures can firstly be divided into wet rice culture and upland rice culture. The two methods of wet rice culture are direct sowing and seedling transplantation. There are two methods of direct sowing, depending on whether the surface of the paddy field is dry or flooded at the time when the seeds are sown.

**Figure 6-18. The position of IRDF in world rice cultures**

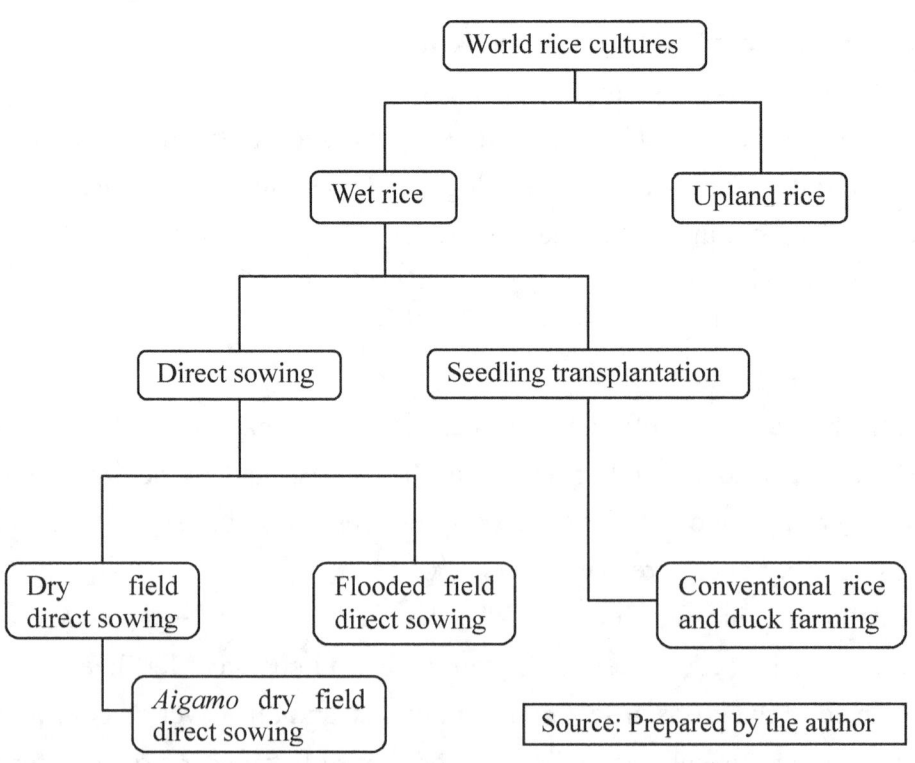

Naturally, almost all conventional IRDF is a technology premised on seedling transplantation. Furthermore, all 'rice cultures that do not use herbicides,'[32] golden snail, tadpole shrimp, rice bran, and winter flooding, with the exception of cloth mulch cultivation, are all techniques based on seedling transplantation.

In seedling transplantation,[33] large seedlings prepared in advance in a seedling nursery are transplanted to a paddy field which has been appropriately flooded with water, and this is a technique that gains an advantage over weeds right from the outset.

Further, flooding originally suppressed the occurrence of weeds. In his book *Paddy Field Soil Science*, Professor Takehiko Yoshida states, "The amount of weeds that occur under conditions of flooding are reduced to about one-third of that occurring in a moist condition of moisture saturation and about one-sixth of that in normal field conditions. There is an especially remarkable reduction in the C4 type weeds that exhibit strong competitiveness with wet rice (hairy finger-grass [*Digitaria ciliaris*] and *hie*)" [119]. In other words, the main purpose of seedling transplantation is flooding for weed suppression.

However, the seedling transplantation method is not the sole rational technique for rice cultivation. In his book *The History of Rice in Asia*, Professor Kohji Tanaka writes, "The Asian rice cultivation sphere can be divided into three zones, the South Asian zone where direct sowing predominates, the Southeast Asian zone where transplantation and direct sowing are mixed, and the East Asian zone where transplantation predominates" [122].

Japan being in East Asia, where rice cultivation is associated with scenes of seedling transplantation, you will see little other than seedling transplantation, but in India and Bangladesh, in Southern Asia, as a part of the technology of the use of the animal power of cattle, dry-paddy direct seed sowing[34] has been widely carried out. Direct sowing has also been carried out in some areas of East Asia which have relatively poor rainfall, such as the Huabei region of China and North Korea. In other words, direct sowing is one of the world's great rice cultivation systems.

The problem with dry-paddy direct sowing is that the sown rice seeds and the seeds of weeds start out simultaneously. Overcoming this weed problem through a combination of *aigamo* and dry-paddy direct sowing is the theme of this technique.

As we can see from Figure 6-19, the problem is how to suppress weeds during the time when the paddy field is dry, between sowing on 20 May and the point where water is allowed to flood the field on 13 June. It is not that all the weeds that appear during this period are a problem. The upland field weeds that appear during this period will die when the field is flooded. The problem is *hie*. *Hie* can grow both in water and on dry land, and so will continue to grow either in an upland field condition or a flooded condition. Furthermore, since it is of the same plant family as the rice plant, *aigamo* will not eat the *hie* leaves.

---

[32] See *Minkan Inasaku Kenkyujo* (Citizen Rice Cultivation Research Institute) [86] for more details on rice cultures that do not use herbicides.
[33] See Takaya [28] for details on the significance of seedling transplantation.
[34] See Kimoto [21] and Fukuoka [39] for details on dry-field no-till direct sowing cultivation.

**Figure 6-19. Cultivation calendar for *aigamo* dry-paddy direct sowing on the Furuno Farm**

| 1 May | Subsoiler | Dry field |
| | Fertilizer spreading | |
| | Deep ploughing with tractor | |
| 20 May | Dry-paddy direct sowing with wheat sowing machine | |
| 27 May | Germination | |
| 13 June | Paddy field flooded | Flooded field |
| | *Aigamo* released into paddy field | |
| 31 August | *Aigamo* removed from paddy field | |
| 5 October | Harvest | |

Source: Prepared by the author

In other words, the problem is how to suppress the growth of *hie* during the period when the paddy field is dry, or even if it does appear, as mentioned earlier, to keep it within the two-leaf stage where the *aigamo* will deal with it when they are released into the paddy field. Much of the *hie* that grows in paddy fields is known as *tainubie* (*Echinochloa oryzicola* Vasing).

In the book *Full Colour Weed Diagnosis*, published by the Rural Culture Association Japan, Tokuichi Kusanagi writes, "Favourable conditions for the appearance of *tainubie* are areas such as paddy fields and marshy ground at a time when the temperature is continually above 14-15°C on most days. It will appear especially in shallow water. However, since it has a strong demand for water, its appearance will be limited in an upland field condition with little moisture" [23].

Certainly in light of my experience with paddy field rotation, if there is a place in the field where the water drains slowly, *hie* and other weeds will appear there, but not in other places in the same paddy field which are quite dry.

So what is necessary is that we prevent weeds with water when there is water in the field, and prevent weeds by ensuring that the field is dry when there is no water in it.

What can we do to make the dry field dryer? We can take two actions. One is to attach a subsoiler to a tractor and cut 1 cm wide grooves in the soil to a depth of 40-45 cm every 3 m in the field. Another action is to till at a shallow depth of about 5 cm. By carrying out these two tasks, it was found that the dry field dried out much more easily, and the number of weeds appearing in the field in the period 20 May to 13 June was extremely small.

I have named the effect of reducing the number of weeds appearing and delaying the onset of weed appearance by drying out the field 'the dry effect.'

Thus, on the 23rd day after sowing, water is allowed into the dry paddy field. At this point, the rice plant seedlings are showing 2.5 to 3 leaves, but since the direct sowing allows them to develop good root systems in the soil the *aigamo* can be released into the field even at this stage. In *aigamo* dry-paddy direct sowing, the *aigamo* are released into the paddy field at the same time as it is 'flushed' with water. Using this 'flush and release' system, weeds that appear after this point are completely suppressed.

*Aigamo* dry-paddy direct sowing is a technique still in its developmental stages. There are still several issues that need to be addressed: When is the best time to carry out the direct sowing? Should a cultivator be run over the field if large numbers of weeds appear in the dry field period? And so on.

Up to now, however, the tasks of seed sowing for seedlings, seedling production, levelling and muddying, and seedling transplantation have been eliminated, and so the overall workload has become much lighter. I think the labour has been reduced to about one quarter of what it was previously. These are the labour-saving techniques.

I will mention other technical points here.

(1) The timing of the sowing can be about 23 days before the first day when water in the local irrigation channels is scheduled to flow. It is important that at the time of sowing the soil in the paddy field should be dry. When cultivating the soil with a tractor, the ideal state is that the soil should be broken up finely so that it resembles the crumbly soil in rice seedling trays.

(2) Germination of the rice seed should be stimulated and the seed stored in paper bags in a refrigerator at about $5^{\circ}$C. The seed will then be ready for sowing anytime you need it. In addition, since there is a temperature difference between the air temperature and the temperature in the refrigerator, the seeds will germinate as soon as they are sown. That will give them an advantage in the competition with the weeds.

(3) In a test comparing early rice and late ripening rice varieties carried out in 2006, even though they were sown on the same day the early-ripening variety budded earlier and grew more quickly.

(4) The sowing depth should be quite deep; 2 to 3 cm. This prevents losses due to sparrows and pigeons.

(5) Keep the soil well tamped down after sowing.

(6) Release *aigamo* into the paddy field a little while after flooding. If you do not do so, the soil around the water inlet will become more easily washed away by the full-time ploughing and muddying effect (F effect).

(7) Since levelling and puddling is not carried out in this technique, water seeps from the paddy field more easily, but this water seepage will be alleviated to some extent by the *aigamo* F effect.

(8) The occurrence of sheath blight disease is surprisingly low with this technique, and perhaps the reason is that levelling and puddling is not carried out in *aigamo* dry-paddy direct sowing.

### 6-12-(3) Direction of future developments – aiming for labour saving with IRDF enclosures

This was how major labour savings were achieved for seed sowing for seedlings, seedling transplantation, levelling and puddling, and seedling transplantation through *aigamo* dry-paddy direct sowing. As a result, setting up and removing the electric fence and the corrugated plastic sheet protecting the levee became a nuisance.

As we can see in Table 6-8, approximately 40 percent of the labour time used in IRDF is actually taken up by work with the nets, posts, and electric fence. This is the most time-consuming part of all the work connected with IRDF.

So from 2005 I decided not to remove the electric fence and corrugated plastic sheet in the autumn and just leave them where they were. The problem was the weeds that grew right beside the plastic sheet. As a countermeasure I developed jointly with Suematsu Denshi Co., Ltd., a company manufacturing electric fences in Yatsushiro City, Kumamoto Prefecture, a grass-mowing machine that would mow weeds only and would not cut the plastic sheet protecting the levee.

Leaving the electric fence and the plastic sheet where they were made the work much easier. Most of all, not having to set up the electric fence within the two-week time limit after seedling transplantation made me far less worried about having to rush to get the work done.

One further method is to enlarge the area enclosed by one enclosure. At one time I enclosed a maximum of 90 ares by enclosing two paddy fields together. Mr. Hong Xiangshao in Heilongjiang Province in China has enclosed five ha with one enclosure. That apparently worked very well.

As I think is clear from everything that has been said above, the difference between traditional duck paddy field grazing and IRDF is enclosure. However, it is also important to work out labour-saving methods for enclosing the fields. This is a task for the future.

### 6-12-(4) 2011: Deep water weed control for dry-paddy direct sowing

2011 was a year of great progress in which I began to see the light at the end of the tunnel of dry-paddy direct sowing technique by submerging the newly germinated rice plants in deep water.

Directly sown rice culture is labour-saving when compared with seedling transplantation rice culture. In direct sowing, however, since the rice plants and weeds start out together, strongly competitive weed plants, especially amphibious wild millets (*nobie*), are likely to overwhelm the rice plants. The main issue in directly sown organic rice is weed control. I have continued to struggle with this structural problem along with my friends, the *aigamo*.

In 2011, I completely changed my way of thinking and I am now engaged in a new endeavour. I had heard from a Brazilian agricultural extension centre director who visited me at my home that newly germinated rice plants can be completely submerged for a few days, and that this was a very effective method of weed control. I was sceptical because I had never thought it was realistic to completely submerge the small rice plants, but after carrying out a few small-scale experiments it seemed that the technique might work. In my area, rice plants germinate about 4 to 7 days after direct sowing on line in a dry paddy. When germination was observed to have taken place all around the paddy, water was allowed into the dry paddy and the rice shoots completely submerged to a depth of 5 to 10 cm. This condition was maintained for 3 to 4 days.

The water was then quickly drained from the paddy until a shallow depth of 0.5 to 1 cm of water remained. The wild millet almost completely flopped over and lodged, but the rice plants stood up straight and firm. The roots of the wild millet were underdeveloped, but the rice put out strong roots. This is due to the difference in the size of the seeds.

20 *aigamo* ducklings per 1000m$^2$ were then released into the paddies. The happy ducklings swam freely about between the rice plants, sown on line at 21 cm intervals, eating up the soft leaves of the weeds and insect pests. The *aigamo* do not eat wild millet plants, but being unable to develop roots due to submergence in deep water and having grown long, soft stems, they floated to the surface of the water after having been trampled and stirred up by the *aigamo*. This technology is adaptable not only to spot sowing and row sowing, but also to random sowing.

I increased the depth of the water in accordance with the growth of the rice plants and the *aigamo*. When the rice ears appeared in mid or late August, the *aigamo* were removed from the paddies. As a result, with the exception of places in the paddies where the paddy floor is high (e.g. near the corners of the paddy field) and therefore not completely submerged, wild millet did not appear and the rice ripened beautifully. The result was no better, but no worse, than the almost complete seedling transplantation *aigamo* paddy technology. The *aigamo* ate all the weed plants such as *konagi* (*Monochoria vaginalis* (var. plantaginea)), *azena* (*Lindernia procumbens* (Krock) Borbas) and *urikawa* (*Sagittaria pygmaea* Miq.).

Deep water submergence is an almost universal technology that can probably be adapted widely to organic rice culture. In *aigamo* dry-paddy direct sowing, it will now be necessary for me to investigate, for example, when it is most effective to begin and end the deep water period. I am also wondering whether it would be possible to extend this technique to seedling transplantation by completely submerging the newly-transplanted seedlings. At any event, it looks like I will have plenty of opportunities to enjoy developing these techniques, and I hope you will too!

# Chapter 7
## A Final Summary

In IRDF thus far I have constructed a technology by a comparison with, and with a critical awareness of, modernized rice cultivation techniques. The notion of 'enclosure' has always been 'obvious' and thus has almost never been studied.

In this work, I have for the first time conducted comparative research involving the IRDF that I advocate and the European agricultural revolution, traditional Asian agriculture, traditional Asian duck paddy field grazing, and Asian IRDF. This has been a diachronic and synchronic comparison based on farming system theory. In other words, it constitutes historical and contemporary comparative research in farming system theory.

As a result, the significance of 'enclosure' has become very distinct in terms of farming system theory. This viewpoint would probably not have arisen simply through a conventional comparison with modernized rice cultivation techniques.

From the perspective of the significance of 'enclosure' in Asian traditions, although there is a great diversity in traditional Asian duck paddy field grazing methods, releasing domesticated ducks to graze in unenclosed paddy fields during the day and taking them home in the evening is something they all have in common. In this case the ducks move freely from paddy field to paddy field in search of food. Conversely, in IRDF, a paddy field in which rice seedlings are standing is enclosed by a net and/or an electric fence and *aigamo* ducklings are released to graze in this limited space. Thus the technical difference between what was the general Asian duck-raising method, traditional duck paddy field grazing, and IRDF is 'enclosure.'

Looked at from the point of view of the constituent factors of productive power, in agriculture these are human labour and the means of production. The means of production can be divided into the means of labour and the objects of labour. Traditional duck paddy field grazing also makes use of the 'animal-powered means of labour' of the duck, but in IRDF the 'container-like means of labour' – the enclosed paddy field – makes possible and supplements the remarkable role of the *aigamo* – the animal-powered means of labour. A deeper comprehension of rice cultivation and livestock breeding in a more integrated way helps us to see that human labour, which makes strategic use of the principle of 'integrated cultivation,' is also indispensible. As a result, the degree, homogeneity, timeliness and continual nature of the six effects of *aigamo* on the rice plant (weed control, insect pest control, nutrient provision, stimulus, the full-time ploughing and muddying effect, and golden snail control) are greatly enhanced.

Looked at from the point of view of human labour, the six *aigamo* effects do not appear through human management, and the important point is that the *aigamo* effects are naturally exhibited in a comprehensive and timely manner as the rice and the *aigamo* grow up together. It is indeed this 'super system' itself that is the most effective result of enclosure.

The European agricultural revolution was established on the basis of a deployment of an advanced land use system that fused together crop rotations and livestock breeding by raising animals in animal sheds, and an advanced, animal-powered plough cultivation system.

In contrast, IRDF, by enclosing the paddy field, developed a principle of integration that fused rice plants and *aigamo* together for their simultaneous and mutual benefit. The result was that, despite the advanced form of land use, IRDF became an integrated technological system combining both the 'labour-saving nature' of Europe's agricultural revolution on the one hand and the 'diversity' of Asian traditional agriculture brought about by its advanced land use on the other.

Seen from the historical perspective of Asian duck grazing, China in the 1960s and Vietnam and the Philippines in the 1970s began to use large amounts of pesticides and chemical fertilizers, causing traditional duck paddy field grazing to recede. From around 2000, nevertheless, IRDF was introduced in Japan and spread to other Asian countries. In other words, looking at the continuity of the history of Asian duck grazing, we can say that traditional Asian duck paddy field grazing has been revived in recent years and has evolved into IRDF through 'enclosure.'

Since the *aigamo* is a small livestock animal, the European agricultural revolution and the development of the advanced plough cultivation system that led to the modernization of agriculture was not necessary. However, the integrated development of the internal relations of living things found in paddy fields all over Asia – rice plants, waterfowl, aquatic plants, and paddy field fish – created an 'integrated farming' principle that rivalled crop rotations by the use of 'enclosure' and brought about a rediscovery of traditional Asian agriculture. If we think about it, we can see the 'Asian paddy field' itself as a 'container-like means of labour' whose function has been enhanced by 'enclosure.'

This completes the story of the uniqueness and universality of IRDF as seen from the viewpoint of farming system theory.

**Japanese Bibliography** (Numbers in square brackets in footnotes, etc. refer to the numbers of the entries below)

引用・参考文献

ア

[1] 「アヒルに関する座談會 (1)」『畜産の研究』第 2 巻第 2 号，養賢堂，1948.

[2] 「アヒルに関する座談會 (2)」『畜産の研究』第 2 巻第 3 号，養賢堂，1948.

[3] 飯沼二郎『農業革命論』未来社，1967，pp154～192.

[4] 衣川義雄『水禽飼養法』養賢堂，1931.

[5] 井上憲一「合鴨水稲経営の阻害要因と今後の展開方向―山口県を事例として―」山口大学卒業論文，1994.

[6] 井上憲一・糸原義人「合鴨稲作の技術と経済性に関する一考察―山口県下における事例分析をふまえて―」『農林業問題研究』第 35 巻第 1 号，1999.

[7] 岩片磯雄『農業経営通論』養賢堂，1971，pp20～74.

[8] 岩片磯雄『有畜経営論』農山漁村文化協会，1982.

[9] 岩本泉「農業経営の成長と経営政策の課題」『農業経営研究』第 35 巻第 4 号 1998，pp4～12.

[10] 江頭和彦・井上善之・辻貴子・田嶋文暁・古野隆雄「合鴨による水田土壌の物理的攪拌について」『日本土壌肥料學雑誌』第 72 巻第 2 号，2001，pp271～273.

[11] 江頭和彦・田嶋文暁・辻貴子・井上善之・古野隆雄「合鴨水稲作水田の自己循環型窒素収支」『日本土壌肥料學雑誌』第 71 巻第 5 号，2000，pp695～696.

[12] 太田保夫『植物ホルモンを生かす』農山漁村文化協会，1987，p51.

[13] 岡重蔵「アヒル」『これからの畜産―農政評論編―』毎日新聞社，1951.


カ

[14] 加用信文『日本農法論』お茶の水書房，1972.

[15] 片野修『ナマズはどこで卵を産むのか』創樹社，1998.

[16] 岸田芳朗・島谷直幸「合鴨水稲同時作における 0 日齢ヒナ放飼の可能性」『有機農業研究年報』第 5 巻，2005，pp170～181.

[17] 藤栄剛・井上憲一・岸田芳朗「合鴨稲作農家の作付行動：危険回避と経験効果」『農業経営研究』第 43 巻第 1 号，2005，pp1～11.

[18] 岸田芳朗・益田孝志「総合技術としてのアゾラ―合鴨水稲同時作に関する農業生産システム―(4)アゾラ―合鴨―土壌―水稲間における窒素の動態」『総合農学』第 47 巻第 1・2 号(通号 114)，2000，pp20～24.

[19] 岸田芳朗・宇都宮尚子「総合技術としてのアゾラ―合鴨水稲同時作に関する農業生産システム―(2) 合鴨の行動特性に及ぼすアゾラの影響」，『総合農学』，第 46 巻第 1 号，1998，pp30～35.

[20] 岸田芳朗・宇都宮尚子「総合技術としてのアゾラ―合鴨水稲同時作に関する農業生産システム―(1) 水稲と合鴨の生産性に及ぼすアゾラの影響」『総合農学』，第 46 巻第 1

号，1998，pp30〜35.

　［21］木本英照・岡武三郎・冨久保男『乾田不耕起』農山漁村文化協会，1995

　［22］桐谷圭治・中筋房夫『害虫とたたかう―防除から管理へ―』日本放送出版協会，1977.

　［23］草薙得一『原色　雑草の診断』農山漁村文化協会，1986，2p

　［24］久米小十郎『アヒルの飼い方』養賢堂，1953.

　［25］久米小十郎「アヒルの水田放飼による駆蟲・除草とその要領」『畜産の研究』，第6巻第4号，養賢堂，1952.


サ

　［26］佐藤喜一・園田立信・長谷川信美「合鴨水稲同時作における合鴨のヒト馴れに関する研究」『日本家畜管理学会誌』第39巻第1号，2003，pp64〜65.

　［27］梅崎輝尚・蔭東清一・内川昌彦・園田立信・「接触刺激が水稲の草型に及ぼす影響」『日本作物学会九州支部会報』第62巻，1996，pp41〜42.

タ

　［28］高谷好一『米をどう捉えるか』NHKブックス，日本放送出版協会，1990.

　［29］高山耕二「合鴨農法からみた薩摩鴨の持つ能力」『合鴨通信』第23巻，1998，pp4〜6.

　［30］辻雅男『アジアの農業近代化を考える〜東南アジアと南アジアの事例から〜』九州大学出版会，2004.

　［31］唐木力『アジア型有機農業のすすめ』農山漁村文化協会，1994.


ナ

　［32］中岡哲郎『自然と人間のための経済学』朝日出版社，1977.

　［33］中筋房夫『総合的害虫管理学』養賢堂，1997.

　［34］那波邦彦『ウンカ―おもしろい生態とかしこい防ぎ方―』農山漁村文化協会，1994.

　［35］根元久『天敵利用と害虫管理』農村漁村文化協会，1995.


ハ

　［36］廣谷陽一・野村新一郎・神尾克二「アヒルの水田放飼試験」『畜産の研究』第3巻第3号，養賢堂，1949.

　［37］廣谷陽一「アヒルの水田放飼とその要領（問）」『畜産の研究』第3巻第11号，養賢堂，1949.

　［38］廣谷陽一，「アヒルの水田放飼の開始時期（問）」，『畜産の研究』、第7巻第8号，養賢堂，1953.

［39］福岡正信『自然農法ー緑の哲学の理論と実践』時事通信社，1976.

［40］胡柏「生産性追求は環境保全と相容れないのかー環境保全型農業への移行に向けた理論視座の確率を求めてー」『農林業問題研究』第158号，2005、pp24～33.

［41］藤栄剛・井上憲一・岸田芳朗「合鴨稲作農家の作付行動ー危険回避と経験効果ー」『農業経営研究』第43巻第1号，2005，pp1～11.

［42］胡柏「環境保全型稲作の収益形成力と形成条件分析ー九州地域を事例としてー」，『農業経営研究』第73巻第1号，2001，pp1～15.

［43］古野隆雄『無限に拡がる　アイガモ水稲同時作』農山漁村文化協会，1997.

［44］古野隆雄『合鴨ばんざいーアイガモ水稲同時作の実際ー』農山漁村文化協会，1992.

［45］古野隆雄『アジア型有機農業のすすめ』農山漁村文化協会，1994.

［46］古野隆雄「ウンカはアイガモ君にお任せください」『現代農業』第85巻6号（通号716），2005，pp253～255.

［47］古野隆雄「直播+アイガモーコツは土を乾かすことー」『現代農業』第84号第12巻，（通号710），2005,pp144～148.

［48］古野隆雄「浅耕・部分耕・鎮圧で変わった　乾田直播の抑草に、転作野菜にー田を乾かす効果絶大！サブソイラ・プラソイラー」『現代農業』第84巻第10号（通号708），2005，pp82～85.

［49］古野隆雄「直播+アイガモ大成功！の秘密　乾かすことで草を出さない『ドライ理論』」『現代農業』第83号第11巻（通号697），2004,132～136.

［50］古野隆雄「ダイコンサルハムシ・コオロギ」『現代農業』第83巻第6号，（通号692），2004，pp215～217.

［51］古野隆雄，「アイガモ君と描く水田農業ビジョン」『現代農業』第83巻第3号（通号689），2004，pp316～319.

［52］古野隆雄「続々アイガモ水稲同時作（27 最終回）アイガモ君とともに、ますますおもしろい農業を」『現代農業』第83巻第1号（通号687），2004，pp130～133.

［53］古野隆雄「続続アイガモ水稲同時作（26）『魚の湧く田んぼ』へ、また一歩」『現代農業』第82巻第12号（通号686），2003，pp138～141.

［54］古野隆雄「続々アイガモ水稲同時作（25）アゼ波シートを切らない草刈り機の刃/ネズミ戦争その後」『現代農業』第82巻第11号（通号685），2003，pp124～127.

［55］古野隆雄「続続アイガモ水稲同時作（24）どうやら成功のようです『直播+アイガモ』」『現代農業』第82巻第9)号（通号683），2003，pp150～153.

［56］古野隆雄「カラスにテグス--外敵防御は実害を与えることが肝心」『現代農業』第82巻第9号（通号683），2003，pp100～102.

［57］古野隆雄「続々アイガモ水稲同時作（23）『直播+アイガモに挑戦！』」『現代農業』第82巻第8号（通号682），2003，pp146～149.

［58］古野隆雄「続々アイガモ（22）省力化も楽しい仕事」『現代農業』第82巻第7号（通

号 681），2003，pp136～139.

[59] 古野隆雄「続々アイガモ(21)アイガモの品種について」『現代農業』現代農業第 82 号第 5 号（通号 679），2003，pp132～135.

[60] 古野隆雄「続々アイガモ水稲同時作(20)鳥耕再考―耕起・不耕起 もう一つの意 味―」『現代農業』第 82 巻第 4 号（通号 678），2003，pp136～139.

[61] 古野隆雄「続々アイガモ水稲同時作(19)田んぼの中に池を掘る その後」『現代農 業 』第 82 巻第 3 号（通号 677），2003，pp128～131.

[62] 古野隆雄「続々アイガモ水稲同時作(18)米もカモもおいしいのです『アイガモ米 は食味が落ちる』の声について、私が思うこと」『現代農業』第 82 巻 1 号（通号 675）， 2003，pp110～113.

[63] 古野隆雄「続々アイガモ水稲同時作(16)ネズミ撃退簡単電気柵」『現代農業 』第 81 巻第 12 号（通号 673），2002，pp132～135.

[64] 古野隆雄「続々アイガモ水稲同時作(15)田んぼはドジョウを待っている」『現代 農業』第 81 巻第 10 号（通号 671），2002，pp132～135.

[65] 古野隆雄「続々アイガモ水稲同時作(14)アイガモ田のチッソの循環」『現代農業』 第 81 巻第 9 号（通号 670），2002，pp134～137.

[66] 古野隆雄「続々アイガモ水稲同時作(13)魚再生プロジェクト―田んぼの中に、池 を掘る―」『現代農業』第 81 号第 8 巻（通号 669），2002，pp144～147.

[67] 古野隆雄「続々アイガモ水稲同時作(12)アイガモ君、アメリカへ飛ぶ」『現代農 業』第 81 巻第 6 号（通号 667），2002，pp130～133.

[68] 古野隆雄「続々アイガモ水稲同時作(11)同時作、そして輪作--水田は、イネだけ つくるところじゃない」『現代農業』第 81 巻第 4 号 （通号 665），2002，pp146～149.

[69] 古野隆雄，「続々アイガモ水稲同時作(10)『おいしさ』が環境と農業を守る」，『現 代農業』，第 81 巻第 3 号（通号 664），2002，pp128～131.

[70] 古野隆雄「続々アイガモ水稲同時作(9)イネも大豊作!」『現代農業』第 81 巻第 1 号（通号 662），2002，pp130～133.

[71] 古野隆雄「続々アイガモ水稲同時作(8)ドジョウ再生プロジェクト」『現代農業』 第 80 巻第 13 号（通号 661），2001，pp192～195.

[72] 古野隆雄「続々アイガモ水稲同時作(7)アゾラの魅力と使いこなし」『現代農業』， 第 80 巻第 12 号（通号 660），2001，pp188～191.

[73] 古野隆雄「続々アイガモ水稲同時作(6)アイガモ田んぼの生物多様性とは?」『現 代農業』第 80 巻第 10 号（通号 658），2001，pp199～203.

[74] 古野隆雄「稲作・水田活用続・続アイガモ水稲同時作(5)アイガモは、害虫を益 虫に変える」『現代農業』第 80 巻第 9 号（通号 657），2001，pp190～193.

[75] 古野隆雄「村を元気にする農業『アイガモ水稲同時作』がアジアに広がる」『現 代農業』第 80 巻第 8 号（通号 656），2001，pp323～326.

［76］古野隆雄「続・続 アイガモ水稲同時作(4)改めて、アイガモの雑草防除力について」『現代農業』第 80 巻第 8 号(通号 656)，2001，pp202〜205.

［77］古野隆雄「続々アイガモ水稲同時作(3)刺激効果は、刺激的」『現代農業』第 80 巻第 6 号(通号 654)，2001，pp196〜199.

［78］古野隆雄「続・続アイガモ水稲同時作(2)水田を大きく囲う」『現代農業』第 80 巻第 4 号(通号 652)，2001，pp198〜201.

［79］古野隆雄「続・続 アイガモ水稲同時作(1)愉快!イネとアイガモと魚とイチジクのとれる田」『現代農業』第 80 巻 3 号(通号 651)，2001，pp206〜209.

［80］古野隆雄「アイガモもアゾラも魚もいる田んぼは、地力まで上がる」『現代農業』第 79 巻第 1 号(通号 636)，2000，pp154〜157.

［81］古野隆雄「ヒエの種調べでわかったアイガモ君は表層の草の種を減らす一種の出芽深度は意外と浅い―」『現代農業』第 78 巻第 6 号(通号 629)，1999，pp234〜236.

［82］古野隆雄「続・アイガモ水稲同時作 3-1 カ月で 1000 倍,アゾラ急増殖!!イネは開張,カモはお腹いっぱい」『現代農業』第 74 巻第 9 号，1995，pp188˜191.


マ

［83］牧野博『ドジョウ―養殖から加工・売り方まで―』農山漁村文化協会，1996.

［84］守田志郎『農法―豊かな農業への接近―』農山漁村文化協会，1972.

［85］宮原益次『水田雑草の生態とその防除―水稲作の雑草と除草剤解説―』全国農村教育協会，1992.

［86］民間稲作研究所『除草剤を使わないイネつくり―２０数種の抑草法の選び方・組み合わせ方―』農山漁村文化協会，1999.

［87］高山耕二・田口光・萬田正治・中西良孝「家鴨卵への異なる音刺激が孵化に及ぼす影響」『鹿兒島大學農學部學術報告』第 56 巻，2006，pp45〜49.

［88］高山耕二・平野喜幸・中西良孝・萬田正治「ミャンマー連邦南シャン洲における合鴨(成鴨)の水田放飼が雑草発生，害虫発生ならびに水稲生産に及ぼす影響」『日本家畜管理学会誌』第 39 巻第 4 号,2004，pp143˜150.

［89］魏紅江・高秉大・高山耕二・中西良孝・萬田正治「環境温度が合鴨の雛の体温と発育に及ぼす影響」『日本家畜管理学会誌』第 39 巻第 2 号,2003，pp69˜77

［90］高秉大・高山耕二・中西良孝・萬田正治・松元里志・下田代智英「合鴨による中耕濁水が水田環境ならびに水稲の生育・収量に及ぼす影響」『日本家畜管理学会誌』第 38 巻第 3 号 2002，pp121〜130.

［91］高秉大・中西良孝・萬田正治「合鴨行動を模倣した人為的接触刺激が水稲の生育と収量性に及ぼす影響」『西日本畜産学会報』第 45 巻,2002，pp19〜24.

［92］高秉大・魏紅江・高山耕二・中西良孝・萬田正治・下田代智英・松元里志「合鴨の接触刺激が水稲の生育と収量に及ぼす影響」『日本家畜管理学会誌』第 37 巻第 2 号，2001，

pp69〜74.

[93] 高山耕二・萬田正治・中西良孝・柳田宏一・「家鴨類の産肉性および繁殖能力の品種間差」『日本家畜管理学会誌』第34巻第3号，1999，pp87~93.

[94] 劉翔・高山耕二・山下研人・中西良孝・萬田正治・稲永淳二・松元里志・中釜明紀「アゾラ-合鴨-稲の有機的生産システムにおける水田の pH，水温および土壌化学成分の変化とその肥料効果」『日本家畜管理学会誌』第34巻第2号，1998，pp51~56.

[95] 尾野喜孝・後藤貴文・那須亮・岩元久雄・高山耕二・中西良孝・萬田正治「家鴨類骨格筋の発達と組織化学的特性に及ぼす水田放飼の影響と品種差」『日本家禽学会誌』第35巻第6号1998，pp367〜375.

[96] 劉翔・高山耕二・山下研人・中西良孝・萬田正治・稲永淳二・松元里志・中釜明紀「アゾラ-合鴨-稲の有機的生産システムにおける除草と駆虫効果ならびに合鴨の行動について」『日本家畜管理学会誌』第34巻第1号，1998，pp13〜22.

[97] 高山耕二・劉翔・角井洋子・山下研人・萬田正治・中西良孝・松元里志・中釜明紀・柳田宏一「家鴨類の水田放飼が雑草ならびに害虫発生に及ぼす影響」『日本家畜管理学会誌』第34巻第1号，1998，pp1〜11.

[98] 高山耕二・山下研人・中西良孝・柳田宏一・獄崎亮・萬田正治「合鴨農法における家鴨類の行動特性」『日本家畜管理学会誌』第34巻，1998，pp38〜39.

[99] 高山耕二・角井洋子・浜田智美・松元里志・中釜明紀・中西良孝・萬田正治「合鴨農法における家鴨類の性能比較」『日本家畜管理学会誌』第33巻，1997，pp22〜23.

[100] 萬田正治「アジアにおける農業技術交流・協力の問題点—合鴨農法の経験から—」『日本の科学者』第31巻第3巻，1996，pp132〜135.

[101] 萬田正治「農家の暮らしと環境を守る合鴨農法」『日本家畜管理研究会誌』第31巻，1995，pp22〜25.

[102] 萬田正治他「稲の生育および収量に及ぼす合鴨の水田放飼の影響」『日本家禽学会誌』第30巻6号，1993，pp443〜447.

[103] 中釜明紀・松元里志・萬田正治「合鴨放飼が普通期水稲の生育・収量に及ぼす影響」『日本作物學會紀事』第62巻(別号2)1993，pp15〜16.

[104] 萬田正治他「水田に放飼した合鴨の成長と行動」『日本家禽学会誌』第30巻第5号，1993，pp383〜387.

[105] 萬田正治他「合鴨の水田放飼による雑草および防虫効果」『日本家禽学会誌』第30巻第5号，1993，p365〜370.

[106] 萬田正治「合鴨の水田放飼による雑草および防虫効果」『日本家禽学会誌』第30巻，1993，pp365〜370.

[107] 萬田正治「水田に放飼した合鴨の成長と行動」『日本家禽会誌』第30巻第5号，1993，pp383〜387.

[108] 萬田正治「合鴨水田放飼による雑草および防虫効果」『日本家禽会誌』第30巻第5

号，1993，pp365〜370.

［109］萬田正治「稲の生育および収量に及ぼす合鴨の水田放飼の影響」『日本家禽学会誌』第 30 巻第 6 号，1993，pp443〜447.

［110］萬田正治「水田に放飼した合鴨の成長と行動」『日本家禽学会誌』第 30 巻第 5 号，1993，pp383〜387.

［111］萬田正治「合鴨の水田放飼による除草および防虫効果」『日本家禽学会誌』，第 30 巻第 5 号，1993，pp365〜370.

［112］萬田正治「水田に放飼した合鴨の成長と行動」『日本家禽学会誌』第 30 巻，1993，pp383〜387.

［113］萬田正治「稲の生育および収量に及ぼす合鴨の水田放飼の影響」『日本家禽会誌』，第 30 巻，1993，pp443〜447.

［114］萬田正治「水田に放飼した合鴨の成長と行動」『日本家禽会誌』第 30 巻，1993，pp383〜387.

［115］萬田正治「合鴨の水田放飼による雑草および防虫効果」『日本家禽会誌』第 30 巻，1993，pp365〜370.

［116］萬田正治「稲の生育および収量に及ぼす合鴨の水田放飼の影響」『日本家禽学会誌』第 30 巻，1993，pp443-447.


ヤ

［117］柳田昌秀『アヒル―肥育と採卵の実際―』農山漁村文化協会，1981.

［118］矢野栄二『天敵―生態と利用技術―』養賢堂，2003.

［119］山根一郎『水田土壌学』農山漁村文化協会，1982，p281.

［120］横山利幸「合鴨を利用した水稲栽培の技術的特徴と経営的評価」『農業経営通信』No.178，1993，pp18〜21.


ワ

［121］渡辺恵三『ドジョウ―水田養殖の実際―』農山漁村文化協会，1967.

［122］渡部忠世『稲作文化の現代的課題―学際的理解のために―』「稲のアジア史第 1 巻アジア稲作文化の生態基盤―技術とエコロジー――」，小学館，1987.

［123］高谷好一「アジア稲作の生態構造」『稲のアジア史第 1 巻アジア稲作文化の生態基盤―技術とエコロジー――』小学館，1987.

［124］福井捷朗「エコロジーと技術」『稲のアジア史第 1 巻アジア稲作文化の生態基盤―技術とエコロジー――』小学館，1987.

［125］渡部忠世「稲と米をめぐるアジア的視野」『稲のアジア史第 2 巻アジア稲作文化の展開―多様と統一――』小学館，1987.

［126］渡部忠世「アジア稲作の＜多様の中の統一＞」『稲のアジア史第 2 巻アジア稲作

文化の展開―多様と統一―』小学館，1987.

　[127] 渡部忠世『農業を考える時代―生活と生産の文化を探る―』農山漁村文化協会，
1995, pp112～113, pp136～137.


その他

　[128] ビル・モリソン『パーマカルチャー―農的暮らしの永久デザイン―』農山漁村
文化協会，1993, p31.

　[129] 郭文韜「中国農業の伝統と現代」『中国古代の生物資源保護と生態農業の発展』
農山漁村文化協会，1989.

　[130] 安徽省外国专家局　安徽省农业科学院合编『稲鸭共生–无公害有机鸭米生产新技
术』2004.

　[131] 雷炎・朱自均主编「稲田综合开发」中国农业出版社，1998, pp62～75.

　[132] 金千瑜・禹盛苗・欧阳由男等「中国稲–鸭农作系统发展概况与稲鸭共育技术研究」
『第四届亚洲稲鸭共作研讨会论文集』镇江市科学技术局・镇江市农林局，2004.

　[133] 古野隆雄「干田直播+合鸭的实践研究」『第四届亚洲稲鸭共作研讨会论文集』镇
江市科学技术局・镇江市农林局，2004.

　[134] 张宗炳・曹骥主编『害虫防治：策略与方法』科学出版社，1990.

　[135] 中闵宗殿・彭治富．王潮生主编『国古代农业科技史图说』中国农业博物馆农史
研究室编农业出版社，1989, pp386～390.

　[136] 倪根全主编『梁家勉农史文集』中国农业出版社.

　[137]『人民中国』2月号，2006, p53.

　[138] 包世增『家鴨―自然の生産システム―』.

　[139] 張楷『放牧鴨の食性についての観察と調査』.

　[140]『日本の有機農業』ダイヤモンド社，1989, p12.

　[141] 酒井淳一『農業資源経済論』農林統計協会，1996, p34.

**Appendix 1: Questionnaire Survey**

**Survey on Integrated Rice and Duck Farming (*Dao-ya gongzuo*)**

National *Aigamo* Rice Association
Representative and Facilitator: Takao Furuno

Your name:
Country
Address
Telephone & FAX number:
Integrated rice and duck farming area: Individual or regional                    ha
Number of persons implementing integrated rice and duck farming: Individual or regional
          persons

A. History and origins
1. From about when did integrated rice and duck farming begin in your area?

2. What was the catalyst for starting integrated rice and duck farming?

3. Is traditional duck paddy field grazing (*daotian yangya*) carried out in your region?

4. Do you think that integrated rice and duck farming and traditional duck paddy field grazing are different?

5. In what way are they different (How do they differ)?

6. Have you had any influence from or connection with the Japanese integrated rice and duck farming?

B. Techniques
1. Cultivation calendar
2. What kind of enclosure do you have around your paddy field(s)?
3. How many ducks (*aigamo*) do you release per 10 ares?
4. At what age (in weeks) are the ducklings released into the paddy field(s)?

C. Business management
1. An outline of your farming business
( ) Paddy fields   ( ) Upland fields   ( ) Livestock

124

2. Your areas of integrated rice and duck farming.                    Ha

3. Labour force.          Persons

4. Yield (kg brown rice/10 ares)

| | |
|---|---|
| *Aigamo* fields | kg |
| Conventional fields | kg |

5. Price (per kg brown rice)

| | |
|---|---|
| *Aigamo* fields | kg |
| Conventional fields | kg |

6. Selling price for ducks (*aigamo*)          per duck

7. Number of ducks (*aigamo*) sold          ducks

8. Expenditures

| | Amount | *Aigamo* fields | Conventional fields |
|---|---|---|---|
| Rice plant seedlings | | | |
| Ploughing | | | |
| Seedling Transplantation | | | |
| Compost | | | |
| Fertilizer | | | |
| Pesticides | | | |
| TOTAL | | | |

9. Do you use chemical fertilizers, pesticides or herbicides?   Yes   No

10. If you answered 'Yes', how much do you use?

| | *Aigamo* fields | Conventional fields |
|---|---|---|
| Chemical fertilizers | | |
| Chemical pesticides | | |
| Chemical herbicides | | |
| TOTAL | | |

11. Is weed control by ducks (*aigamo*) sufficient?   Yes   No

12. Types of weeds and approximate time of appearance.

| Type or name of weed | Approximate time or date of appearance |
| --- | --- |
|  |  |
|  |  |
|  |  |

13. What insect pests are there?

14. Is insect pest control by ducks (*aigamo*) alone sufficient?   Yes   No   Don't know

15. When do these insect pests arrive?   Approximately in the month of…

16. Are you aware of the stimulus effect?   Very much so   A little   No   Don't know

17. Method of protection from predators.

18. At night, are the ducks (*aigamo*)

(   ) Kept in the fields

(   ) Kept in a shed

(   ) Taken home

(   ) Other

|  |
| --- |
|  |

19. What are your reasons for choosing the integrated rice and duck farming method form of farm management?

|  |
| --- |
|  |

20. What do you consider to be the best feature of integrated rice and duck farming?

|  |
| --- |
|  |

21. What do you consider to be the weak points of integrated rice and duck farming?

|  |
| --- |
|  |

22. Does integrated rice and duck farming make your work more enjoyable?   Yes   No

**Appendix 2**

Numbers of domesticated birds raised in selected countries

| China | 725,018,000 |
|---|---|
| Indonesia | 34,275,000 |
| Cambodia | 7,000,000 |
| Korea | 5,500,000 |
| Viet Nam | 50,000,000 |

Source: FAOSTAT

**Acknowledgements for the English Version**

In September 2007, I received a Ph.D. by submitting this dissertation to Kyushu University. I have presented all the people who were so generous with their help and advice up to that time with copies of the original Japanese paper. I have also received many warm words of congratulations from a great number of people. Of these, the words that gave me the most joy in my heart were from my aunt, who said, "I read it right to the end!" My aunt has spent her whole life in agriculture since she graduated middle school.

My Ph.D. dissertation represents what has been revealed to me through the work of farming – building up the soil, raising the crops and taking care of the livestock. When writing the paper, I have always tried to be careful to write it in my own words, in a way that anyone can understand it.

I very much hope that this paper will be read by the multitudes of people who, like me, engage in hard work with their minds and bodies from morning till night. I have tried to write it using very plain language and I think it can be read by anyone.

The planning, translation, editing and publishing of the English version of the dissertation has been carried out by Tony Boys and Pat Ormsby, with help from Anna Ono, who reworked many of the figures in the computer.

Finally, I would just like to extend my heartfelt gratitude to everyone for their unstinting assistance and guidance in producing both the original Japanese and the English versions of this paper.

*Aigamo wo*                  The clouds ascend

*Hanshi owareba*            as I finish releasing

*Kumo agaru*                the *aigamo*

Summer, 2012
Takao Furuno

**About the translators:**

**Pat Ormsby** is a full-time professional translator of Japanese to English living in Japan. She can be contacted by email at pat[at]yahoo.com

**Tony Boys** is a full-time professional translator of Japanese to English living in the Japanese countryside. He can be contacted by email at tonbo80[at]hotmail.com

Thanks are also due to Margaret Suzuki for help during the editing phase and to Anna Ono for remaking digital versions of many of the figures.

------------------------------------------------------

*Kindly send questions and comments directly to Takao Furuno at*

furuno@d4.dion.ne.jp

------------------------------------------------------

www.ingramcontent.com/pod-product-compliance
Lightning Source LLC
Chambersburg PA
CBHW081200280526
45788CB00008B/2745